The Squam Lake Report

John H. Cochrane

Douglas W. Diamond

Anil K Kashyap

Raghuram G. Rajan

CHICAGO **BOOTH**

The Squam Lake Group is 15 academics who have come together to offer guidance on the reform of financial regulation.
  Our group first convened in the fall of 2008, amid the deepening capital markets crisis. Although informed by this crisis—its events and the ongoing policy responses—the group is intentionally focused on longer-term issues. We aspire to help guide reform of capital markets—their structure, function, and regulation. We base this guidance on the group's collective academic, private sector, and public policy experience.

Kenneth R. French
Dartmouth College

Martin N. Baily
Brookings Institution

John Y. Campbell
Harvard University

John H. Cochrane
University of Chicago

Douglas W. Diamond
University of Chicago

Darrell Duffie
Stanford University

Anil K Kashyap
University of Chicago

Frederic S. Mishkin
Columbia University

Raghuram G. Rajan
University of Chicago

David S. Scharfstein
Harvard University

Robert J. Shiller
Yale University

Hyun Song Shin
Princeton University

Matthew J. Slaughter
Dartmouth College

Jeremy C. Stein
Harvard University

René M. Stulz
Ohio State University

The Squam Lake Report

Fixing the Financial System

Kenneth R. French, Martin N. Baily, John Y. Campbell,
John H. Cochrane, Douglas W. Diamond, Darrell Duffie,
Anil K Kashyap, Frederic S. Mishkin, Raghuram G. Rajan,
David S. Scharfstein, Robert J. Shiller, Hyun Song Shin,
Matthew J. Slaughter, Jeremy C. Stein, René M. Stulz

PRINCETON UNIVERSITY PRESS

PRINCETON AND OXFORD

Published by Princeton University Press, 41 William Street,
Princeton, New Jersey 08540
In the United Kingdom: Princeton University Press, 6 Oxford Street,
Woodstock, Oxfordshire OX20 1TW
press.princeton.edu

Library of Congress Cataloging-in-Publication Data

The Squam Lake report : fixing the financial system / Kenneth R.
French . . . [et al.].
    p. cm.
Includes index.
    ISBN 978-0-691-14884-7 (hbk. : alk. paper)   1. Financial crises—
Prevention. 2. Finance—Government policy. 3. Capital market—
Government policy. I. French, Kenneth R.
    HB3722.S79 2010
    332.1—dc22

                                      2010009897

British Library Cataloging-in-Publication Data is available

This book has been composed in ITC Garamond Std
Printed on acid-free paper. ∞
Printed in the United States of America

10 9 8 7 6 5 4 3 2

Contents

Preface   vii

Acknowledgments   xi

CHAPTER 1: Introduction   1

CHAPTER 2: A Systemic Regulator for Financial
            Markets   33

CHAPTER 3: A New Information Infrastructure for
            Financial Markets   44

CHAPTER 4: Regulation of Retirement Savings   53

CHAPTER 5: Reforming Capital Requirements   67

CHAPTER 6: Regulation of Executive Compensation
            in Financial Services   75

CHAPTER 7: An Expedited Mechanism to
            Recapitalize Distressed Financial
            Firms: Regulatory Hybrid Securities   86

CHAPTER 8: Improving Resolution Options for
            Systemically Important Financial
            Institutions   95

CHAPTER 9: Credit Default Swaps, Clearinghouses,
            and Exchanges   109

CHAPTER 10: Prime Brokers, Derivatives Dealers,
and Runs   122

CHAPTER 11: Conclusions   135

List of Contributors   153
Index   157

Preface

The Squam Lake Group is 15 leading financial economists who came together to offer guidance on the reform of financial regulation. The group first met for a weekend in the fall of 2008 at a remote and scenic retreat on New Hampshire's Squam Lake. The World Financial Crisis was then at its peak. Although informed by this crisis—its events and the ongoing policy responses—the group has intentionally focused on longer-term issues. We have aspired to help guide the evolving reform of capital markets—their structure, function, and regulation.

This guidance is based on our collective academic, private sector, and public policy experience. Members include eight of the nine most recent presidents of the American Finance Association (including the current president and the president-elect), a former Federal Reserve Governor, a former Chief Economist of the International Monetary Fund, and former members of the Council of Economic Advisers under President Bill Clinton and President George W. Bush. The group has been united and motivated by a common concern: that policymakers often misunderstand or ignore the large body of academic knowledge that could guide sound regulatory reform, resulting in poorly designed policies with unintended consequences.

After the initial Squam Lake meeting, the group worked to develop specific proposals targeted at policymakers around the world. We collaborated through emails, phone calls, and meetings. The breadth of expertise in the group led to many interesting and sometimes spirited discussions. But all members of the group came to agree on a growing list of urgent and important recommendations. Throughout, the group has been staunchly nonpartisan, with no business or political sponsor.

As agreement was reached on a topic, we crafted a white paper summarizing our analysis and recommendations, and then worked to have it inform policy conversations in real time. Members of the group have been actively engaged in the policy process at the highest level around the world. In the United States, members have briefed Democratic and Republican Senators and Representatives and testified before both chambers of Congress. We have consulted with officials at the Federal Reserve Board, the Federal Reserve Bank of New York, the Treasury Department, the Council of Economic Advisers, the European Central Bank, the Bank for International Settlement, and the Securities and Exchange Commission, and with the President of Korea. Members of the group have also made presentations at the Bank of England, Her Majesty's Treasury, the Banque de France, and the European Commission, and we have had meetings with individual policymakers from many other countries.

This book collects and briefly explains the group's policy recommendations. The introduction highlights features of the World Financial Crisis that shaped our recommendations and previews connections among all of them. Subsequent chapters present our proposals on specific issues. The concluding chapter describes two key principles that summarize our proposals and explores how these proposals would have mitigated the World Financial Crisis. Finally, we discuss some challenges that may impede the adoption of our proposals.

Acknowledgments

The group warmly thanks Peter Dougherty and Seth Ditchik of Princeton University Press for their interest in creating this book, their keen oversight of its speedy production, and their support for its innovative distribution. We thank Wendy Simpson for her expertise in arranging all logistics for the initial meeting on Squam Lake, and Andy Bernard for suggesting we should form the group and for his contributions during our first meeting. Our individual white papers were originally disseminated by the Council on Foreign Relations. We thank Sebastian Mallaby at CFR for his ongoing guidance and support; for editorial input we also thank his CFR colleagues Lia Norton and Patricia Dorff.

The group wishes to recognize the special efforts of Ken French, who has served as the leader and coordinator of our collected efforts and is therefore listed as first author, and of Matt Slaughter, who made extraordinary contributions during the drafting of the text. The members of the group also thank our families, who patiently supported and tolerated many long days and late nights. Finally, the group recognizes the large debt it owes to the many financial economists, both inside and outside academia, who have contributed to the body of knowledge from which we have drawn.

The Squam Lake Report

Chapter 1

Introduction

The financial system promotes our economic welfare by helping borrowers obtain funding from savers and by transferring risks. During the World Financial Crisis, which started in 2007 and seems to have ebbed as we write in 2010, the financial system struggled to perform these critical tasks. The resulting turmoil contributed to a sharp decline in economic output and employment around the globe.

The extraordinary policy interventions during the Crisis helped stabilize the financial system so that banks and other financial institutions could again support economic growth. Though the Crisis led to a severe downturn, a repeat of the Great Depression has so far been averted. The interventions by governments around the world have left us, however, with enormous sovereign debts that threaten decades of slow growth, higher taxes, and the dangers of sovereign default or inflation.

How do we prevent a replay of the World Financial Crisis? This is one of the most important policy questions confronting the world today, and it remains unanswered. In this book, we offer recommendations to strengthen the financial system and thereby reduce the likelihood of such damaging episodes. Though informed by the lessons of the Crisis, our proposals are guided by long-standing economic principles.

When developing our recommendations, we think carefully about the incentives of those who will be affected and about unintended consequences. We try to identify the specific problem to be solved and the divergence between private and social benefits behind that problem; we carefully examine the possible unintended effects of our proposed solution; and we consider ways in which individuals or institutions can circumvent the regulation or capture the regulators.

Two central principles support our recommendations. First, policymakers must consider how regulations will affect not only individual financial firms but also the financial system as a whole. When setting capital requirements, for example, regulators should consider not only the risk of individual banks, but also the risk of the whole financial system. Second, regulations should force firms to bear the costs of failure they have been imposing on society. Reducing the conflict between financial firms and society will cause the firms to act more prudently.

In the remainder of this book we present a series of policy proposals, each of which can be read on its own or in combination with the others. The conclusion summarizes these proposals and shows how they might have helped during the World Financial Crisis.

WHAT HAPPENED IN THE WORLD
FINANCIAL CRISIS?

The Prelude

The first symptoms of the World Financial Crisis appeared in the summer of 2007, as a result of losses on mortgage backed securities. For example, in August, BNP Paribas suspended the redemption of shares in three funds that had invested in these securities, and American Home Mortgage Investment Corp. declared bankruptcy. Mortgage related losses continued throughout the fall, and indicators of stress in the financial system, including the interest rates that banks charge each other, were unusually high. Despite huge injections of liquidity by the U.S. Federal Reserve and the European Central Bank, financial institutions began to hoard cash, and interbank lending declined. Northern Rock was unable to refinance its maturing debt and the firm collapsed in September 2007, becoming the first bank failure in the United Kingdom in over 100 years.

The next big problem was in the market for auction rate securities. Although auction rate securities are long-term bonds, short-term investors found them attractive before the Crisis because sponsoring banks held auctions at regular intervals—typically every 7, 28, or 35 days—to allow the security holders to sell their bonds. Thousands of the auctions failed in February 2008 when the number of owners who wanted to sell their bonds exceeded the number of bidders who wanted to buy them at the maximum rate allowed by the bond and, unlike in previous auctions, the sponsoring banks did not absorb the surplus. After much litigation, the major sponsoring banks agreed to pay many of their clients' losses. The market for auction rate securities has not revived.

Bear Stearns' failure in March 2008 proved, in retrospect, a critical turning point. The firm had funded much of its operations with overnight debt, and when it lost a lot of money on mortgage backed securities, its lenders refused to renew that debt. At the same time, customers ran from its prime brokerage business, a process we describe in detail below. Over the weekend of March 15, the U.S. government brokered a rescue by J.P. Morgan that included a generous commitment by the Federal Reserve. Many observers and officials thought that the Crisis was contained at this point and that markets would police credit risks aggressively. That hope proved unfounded.

The Remarkable Month of September 2008

The World Financial Crisis moved into an acute phase in September 2008.[1] Fannie Mae and Freddie Mac, large government-sponsored enterprises that create, sell, and speculate on mortgage backed securities, failed during the first week of September and were placed under the conservatorship of the Federal Housing Finance Agency.

The peak of the Crisis started on Monday, September 15, 2008. Lehman Brothers, a brokerage and investment bank headquartered in New York, failed with a run by its short-term creditors and prime brokerage customers that was similar to the run experienced by Bear Stearns. Lehman's bankruptcy was a surprise, since the government had stepped in to prevent the bankruptcy of Bear Stearns only months before.

Within days, the U.S. government rescued American International Group. AIG had written hundreds of billions of dollars of credit default swaps, which are essentially insurance contracts that pay off when a specific borrower, such as a corporation, or a specific security, such as a bond, defaults. As economic conditions worsened and it became increasingly likely that AIG would have to pay off on at least some of its commitments, the swap contracts required the firm to post collateral with its counterparties. AIG was unable to make the required payments. Goldman Sachs was AIG's most prominent counterparty, and Goldman's demands for collateral were an important part of AIG's demise. The cost to taxpayers of government assistance for Fannie Mae, Freddie Mac, and AIG is now projected at hundreds of billions of dollars.

That same week, Treasury Secretary Hank Paulson announced the first Troubled Asset Relief Program (TARP), asking Congress for $700 billion to buy mortgage backed securities. Federal Reserve Chairman Ben Bernanke and President George W. Bush also gave important speeches warning of grave danger to the financial system. The Securities and Exchange Commission banned the short-selling of several hundred financial stocks, causing pandemonium in the options market, which relies on short-selling to hedge positions, and among hedge funds that employed long-short strategies.[2]

The turmoil of the week did not stop there. Interbank lending declined sharply, the commercial paper market slowed to a crawl, and there was a run on the Reserve Primary Fund, a money market mutual fund. Unlike other mutual funds, money market funds maintain a constant share price, typically $1, by using profits in the fund to pay interest rather than to increase share values. Because the share price is fixed at $1, losses that push a fund's net asset value below $1 per share can trigger a run, as investors rush to claim their full dollar payments and force the losses onto other investors. The Reserve Primary Fund, which had more than 1 percent of its assets in commercial paper issued by Lehman, suffered just such a run on September 16, 2008. After Lehman declared bankruptcy, the fund's net asset value dropped to $0.97 per share and investors withdrew more than two-thirds of the Reserve Fund's $64 billion in assets before the fund suspended redemptions on September 17. Concern spread to investors in other money market funds, and they withdrew almost 10 percent of the $3.5 trillion invested in U.S. money market funds over the next ten days. To stabilize the market, the government took the unprecedented step of offering a guarantee to every U.S. money market fund.

In normal times, any one of these events would have been the financial story of the year, yet they all happened in the same week in September 2008. Although much commentary and popular press coverage blames the World Financial Crisis entirely on the government's decision to let Lehman fail, such an analysis ignores the evident contributions of the many other momentous events that occurred during that week.

October 2008: The Bank Bailout and Credit Crunch

By early October 2008, the U.S. government realized that the TARP plan to buy mortgage backed securities on the open market was not feasible. Instead, the Treasury Department used the appropriated money to purchase preferred stock in large banks, and to provide credit guarantees and other support. Though now remembered as the "bank bailout," the TARP purchases were not simply a transfer to failing institutions. Healthy banks were also forced to accept capital in an attempt to mask the government's opinions about which banks were in more trouble than others. Many policymakers seemed to think that banks were not lending because they had lost too much capital and were not able or willing to raise more. Thus, the goal seemed to be not to save the banks but to recapitalize them so they would lend again. In the end, the former result was achieved—none of the large banks that received TARP funds failed—but the latter, arguably, was not. We analyze these issues in detail below, and recommend some alternative structures and policies that we believe would have worked better.

During much of the World Financial Crisis, the Federal Reserve experimented with a wide range of new facilities beyond its traditional tools of interest rate policy and open market operations. The Fed lent broadly to commercial banks, investment banks, and broker-dealers, and ended up buying commercial paper, mortgages, asset backed securities, and long-term government debt in an effort to lower interest rates in these markets. By December 2008, excess reserves in the banking system had grown from $6 billion before the Crisis to over $800 billion. These actions are not a focus of our analysis, but they surely helped prevent the Crisis from turning into another Great Depression. At a minimum, they eliminated most banks' concerns about sources of cash.

Bank failures in Europe in the fall of 2008 led to more direct bailouts. The Netherlands, Belgium, and Luxembourg spent $16 billion to prop up Fortis, a major European bank with about $1 trillion in assets. The Netherlands spent $13 billion to bail out ING, a banking and insurance giant. Germany provided a $50 billion rescue package for Hypo Real Estate Holdings. Switzerland rescued UBS, one of the ten largest banks in the world, with a $65 billion package. Iceland took over its three largest banks, and its subsequent difficulties highlight what happens when the cost of bailing out a country's banks exceeds the government's resources.

Throughout the fall of 2008, there was a "flight to quality" in markets around the world. When investors are worried about default, they demand higher interest rates. Yields on securities with any hint of default risk rose sharply, especially in the financial sector.

The flight to quality is apparent in the interest rates on commercial paper, in Figure 1. Commercial paper is short-term unsecured debt issued by banks and other large corporations and is an important part of their financing. The commercial paper rates for financial institutions and lower-credit quality borrowers jumped in September and October, but after a small increase, the rate for large creditwor-

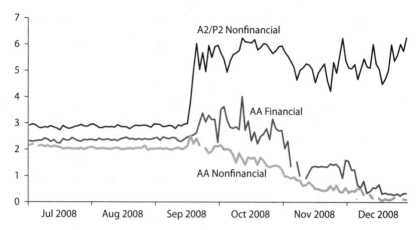

Figure 1: Annualized Percent Yields on 30-Day High-Quality (AA) Financial and Nonfinancial Commercial Paper and Medium-Quality (A2/P2) Nonfinancial Commercial Paper, in Percent, August to December 2008. Source: Federal Reserve

thy nonfinancial companies actually declined. The rate on U.S. Treasury bills, which are viewed as the most secure investment, also fell; the three-month Treasury bill rate actually dropped to zero for brief periods in November and December 2008.

THE RUN ON THE SHADOW BANKING SYSTEM

The panic that struck financial markets in the fall of 2008 has been characterized as a run on the shadow banking system, and with good reason. Before the Crisis, many bonds, mortgage backed securities, and other credit instruments were held by leveraged non-bank intermediaries, including hedge funds, investment banks, brokerage firms, and special-purpose vehicles. Many of these intermediaries were forced to "delever" during October and November, selling assets to repay their creditors.

Hedge funds and other leveraged intermediaries use the securities in their portfolios as collateral when they borrow money. During the World Financial Crisis, many wary lenders decided the collateral borrowers had posted before the Crisis was no longer sufficient to guarantee repayment. When the lenders demanded either more or better collateral, many borrowers were forced to sell their levered positions and repay their loans. The result was a reduction in the quantity of assets they held and in their leverage. In addition, hedge funds and other intermediaries suffered large withdrawals by panicky customers, again forcing them to sell securities on the market. The assets being sold were generally acquired by individual investors, the federal government, or commercial banks, which as a group financed most of their purchases by borrowing from the government.[3]

The financing difficulties faced by arbitrageurs and liquidity providers are apparent in a series of fascinating market pathologies. In financial markets, there are often many different ways to obtain the same outcome. An investor can use many different combinations of securities, for example, to risklessly convert dollars today into dollars in six months. The actions of arbitrageurs usually keep the costs of the different approaches closely aligned. During the fall of 2008, the costs often diverged, with the approach that required more capital typically costing less.[4]

The principle of covered interest parity, for example, says that after eliminating exchange rate risk, risk-free investing should have the same return in every currency. An investor who wants to invest dollars today and receive dollars in the future usually buys a U.S. bond. He could accomplish the same thing by converting his dollars into euros, investing in a riskless euro bond, and locking in the conversion of the euro payoff back into dollars with a forward contract. Since both strategies convert dollars today into dollars in the future, they should have the same return.[5] Suppose instead the return on the U.S. bond is lower. Then an arbitrageur could borrow money in the United States at the lower rate, invest it in the euro transaction at the higher rate, and make a profit.

During the Crisis, covered interest parity violations as large as 20 basis points (0.20 percent) emerged.[6] This may seem trivial, but in normal times these violations rarely exceed 2 basis points. Moreover, traders can usually "lever up" transactions like this and make a large profit. But that's the catch—hedge funds, brokerages, and investment banks were being forced to delever during the Crisis, and 20 basis points is not enough to entice many long-only investors to replace the U.S. bond they are currently holding with a foreign bond and some seemingly complicated currency transactions.

Other recent research finds similar disruptions of the normal pricing relations linking (1) Treasury bonds, corporate bonds, and credit-default swaps (a Treasury bond should be the same as a corporate bond plus a credit default swap—except for liquidity, financing, and CDS counterparty risk); (2) fixed and floating rate investments (a sequence of short-term investments plus a contract swapping a floating interest rate for a fixed interest rate should have the same payoff as a fixed rate investment); (3) convertible bonds, debt, and equity; (4) newly issued "on-the-run" and recently issued "off-the-run" Treasury bonds, which have essentially the same payoff but differ in liquidity; and (5) stock and option prices, which are linked by what financial economists call the put-call parity relation.[7]

The breakdown of these normal pricing relations does little direct harm to the rest of the economy. A 20-basis-point violation of covered interest parity has little effect on a U.S. exporter using currency contracts to lock in the rate at which it can convert future Japanese revenue back into dollars. These violations show, however, that markets were not functioning normally. In particular, they suggest there was not much capital available to provide liquidity to buyers and sellers. Anyone needing to sell securities quickly in such a market—such as a financial institution trying to reduce its risk—was not likely to get a good price.

LENDING, BANKING, AND THE RECESSION

During the fall of 2008, output and financing activity contracted sharply. Commercial paper, corporate bond, and equity issuance all fell dramatically, as did mortgage originations.

Originations of most types of asset backed securities also slowed to a trickle. Many banks in the United States

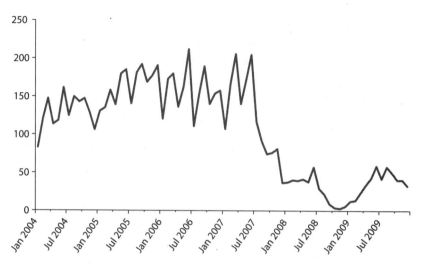

Figure 2: Asset Backed Securities Issued in the United States, January 2004 to December 2009, Billions of Dollars per Month. Source: Federal Reserve

and other countries no longer hold much of the credit they issue. They have moved instead to an "originate and sell" model in which they bundle together similar loans, such as jumbo mortgages, commercial loans, student loans, or credit card debt, and sell them to investors as asset backed securities. New issues of these securities essentially stopped in October and November 2008. Figure 2 shows that the amount of asset backed securities issued in the United States rose from $28.8 billion in January 2000 to $385.3 billion in June 2007, and then plunged to $102.6 billion in September 2007. Issuance in the United States continued to decline over the next year, eventually falling to only $8.7 billion in October 2008 and $6.6 billion in

November—just 2 percent of the volume 18 months earlier. Only mortgages pooled by Fannie Mae and Freddie Mac, with an explicit government guarantee and subject to huge Federal Reserve purchases, continued to flow to the market.

There is plenty of anecdotal and survey evidence that bank lending also dried up during the Crisis. For example, loan officers surveyed by the Federal Reserve reported that credit conditions progressively tightened during 2008. In a survey about their perceptions of credit conditions and corporate decisions as of late November 2008, more than half of the chief financial officers of large American firms who responded said that their firms were either "somewhat or very affected by the cost or availability of credit."[8]

There is a lively and fundamentally important debate about why the quantity of lending fell. Some financial economists argue that banks wanted to lend more but were unable to do so because they faced binding capital constraints. In this view, information costs and other frictions in the loan origination process kept customers from moving to less constrained banks.

Others argue that the primary reason banks were unwilling to lend is that their customers had become less creditworthy. These economists point out that the high level of uncertainty about future economic conditions during the Crisis ratcheted up the default risk of even the most reliable clients. This interpretation of the decline in bank lending implies that no amount of capital would have induced banks as a group to lend more because all the good loans were being made.

Figure 3 shows data on the quantity of bank lending

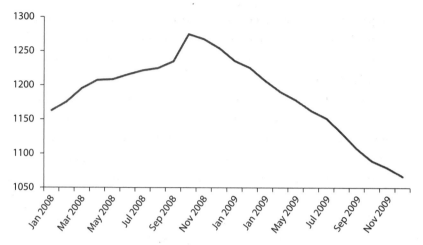

Figure 3: Commercial and Industrial Loans by U.S. Commercial Banks, 2008–9, in Billions of Dollars. Source: Federal Reserve

in the United States in 2008 and 2009. Starting in October 2008 there was a spike in lending, followed by a protracted decline. V. V. Chari, Lawrence Christiano, and Patrick Kehoe take the spike at face value: in aggregate, banks lent more. At a minimum, the banking system as a whole—as opposed to individual banks—was not deleveraging to overcome loss of capital.[9] Victoria Ivashina and David Scharfstein note that much of the increase in bank lending was involuntary on the part of the banks, the result of drawdowns by borrowers on existing lines of credit.[10] They also show that banks that were more vulnerable to drawdowns because they were in more syndicates with Lehman reduced subsequent lending more, and conclude that there was indeed a genuine contraction in the effective supply of bank credit.

Economists will argue about the events of the World Financial Crisis for years to come. In fact, we still argue about the Great Depression. None of the analysis behind our recommendations, however, depends on how these debates are settled. For example, no matter how capital-constrained the banking system really was in the fall of 2008, our proposals for changes that make such constraints less binding and give policymakers better tools when they fear capital constraints remain valid.

WHAT WAS WRONG WITH THE FINANCIAL SYSTEM DURING THE CRISIS?

The Crisis revealed a number of serious problems with our financial system. Some had been in the background all along, others did not appear until the Crisis. In this book we emphasize four categories of problems: conflicts of interest, known to economists as agency problems; the difficulty of applying standard bankruptcy procedures to financial institutions; the emergence of a modern form of bank runs; and the inadequacy of the regulatory structure, which had not kept up with recent financial innovation. (In fact, much innovation served to escape regulations.)

Conflicts of Interest: Agency Problems

Conflicts of interest that cannot be resolved easily by contracts or markets occur throughout the economy, but they can be particularly harmful in the financial system. There are several reasons. First, many financial transactions and contracts involve a principal, such as an investor or shareholder, asking a trader, manager, or other agent to act on his or her behalf. Second, most financial transactions involve highly uncertain future payoffs, and in many transactions one party is better informed about the payoffs than the other. Third, the high volatility of the future payoffs often makes it hard to assess whether the outcome of a financial transaction is due to the agent's efforts or luck. And fourth, the sums involved can be huge.

Some proprietary traders, for example, earn a lot when their trades do well, but their personal losses are limited when their trades do poorly. Because of the asymmetric nature of their compensation, these traders can increase their expected income by taking riskier positions. This problem is dramatically illustrated by periodic cases in which "rogue traders" incur losses that are big enough to damage or even destroy large financial institutions. In 1995 Nick Leeson brought down Barings Bank with a $1.3 billion loss, and in 2008 it was revealed that Jérôme Kerviel had severely damaged Société Générale with a loss of over $7 billion.

Conflicts of interest, or "agency problems," also exist at many other levels within the financial system. Shareholders of financial institutions have a conflict of interest with the bank's senior executives, especially when those executives are rewarded for good performance but do not have a large fraction of their wealth tied up in the shares of the bank.

Many financial institutions have large quantities of debt,

which creates a conflict of interest between the bank's creditors and its shareholders. Shareholders have an incentive to authorize excessively risky investments, for example, especially after a bank has incurred losses that erode the value of the shareholders' claim. The gains on these risky investments will accrue largely to shareholders, while the losses will mostly be borne by creditors. The conflict with creditors also reduces the incentives for the shareholders of troubled institutions to raise new capital because that would strengthen the position of creditors while diluting the shareholders' position. This "debt overhang" problem was widely cited during the World Financial Crisis, when many banks that were insolvent, or close to insolvency, seemed reluctant either to raise new capital or to reduce their risks by selling distressed securities.[11]

At the highest level, there is a conflict of interest between society as a whole and the private owners of financial institutions. Because robust financial institutions promote economic growth and employment, during financial crises governments often rescue troubled firms they perceive to be systemically important. The result is privatized gains and socialized losses. If things go well, the firms' owners and managers claim the profits, but if things go poorly, society subsidizes the losses.

The candidates for government bailouts are popularly described as "too big to fail." More precisely, the argument for government support—which many economists challenge—is about firms that are too systemically important to fail. In its 2004 Annual Report, the European Central Bank described systemic risk as "The risk that the inability of one institution to meet its obligations when due will cause other institutions to be unable to meet their obligations when due. Such a failure may cause significant liquidity or credit problems and, as a result, could threaten the stability of or confidence in markets." Systemically important firms are those whose failure could pose a large threat to the stability of or confidence in markets. These firms are likely to be large, but they also tend to have complex interconnections with other financial institutions.

Too-big-to-fail policies offer systemically important firms the explicit or implicit promise of a bailout when things go wrong. These policies are destructive, for several reasons. First, because the possibility of a bailout means a firm's stakeholders claim all the profits but only some of the losses, financial firms that might receive government support have an incentive to take extra risk. The firm's shareholders, creditors, employees, and management all share the temptation. The result is an increase in the risks borne by society as a whole.

Second, these policies encourage smaller financial institutions to expand or to become more closely interconnected with other firms, so they move under the too-big-to-fail umbrella. Firms have an incentive to do whatever it takes to make policymakers fear their failure, creating the very fragility the government wishes to avoid. Belief that a government rescue will protect a financial institution's creditors in a crisis also gives a firm a competitive advantage, lowering its cost of financing and allowing it to offer better prices to its customers than its fundamental productivity warrants.

Third, inefficient firms that cannot compete on their own should fail. Otherwise, firms have less incentive to become and stay efficient. A government policy that props up inefficient firms is wasteful and destructive. Allowing these firms to fail frees up resources and provides opportunities for more efficient and innovative competitors to flourish.

Fourth, and most generally, capitalism is undermined by policies that privatize gains but socialize losses. Government guaranteed institutions can become government run institutions, allocating credit, for example, to maximize political gain rather than economic welfare.

The conflict between society and the owners of financial firms becomes more serious during severe crises, when many financial institutions are close to insolvent. It is the prime motivation for our regulatory proposals, but several of the lower-level conflicts we have described are relevant because they magnify the risk borne by society as a whole.

The self-serving behavior that many of our recommendations target—whether by traders, senior management, or the firm's owners—need not be strategic, intentionally malicious, or even conscious. Consider a trader who inadvertently develops an investment strategy with highly probable gains and improbable but large losses. Like a firm that has sold earthquake insurance, the strategy may produce a long string of impressive returns before one year of losses wipes out many years of profits.[12] If so, during the good years the trader will be celebrated for his or her brilliance, rewarded with large bonuses, and given more resources to manage. Many sophisticated traders and hedge funds were not aware of the "earthquake risks" inherent in many of their strategies. Similarly, when firms take actions that increase the likelihood of a government bailout in the next financial crisis, the market rewards them with a lower cost of capital. As firms become too big to fail, for example, the implicit government guarantee reduces the riskiness of their debt and lowers the interest rate demanded by their creditors. A CEO working to maximize firm value may not even realize the importance of the government guarantee, but a Darwinian process will encourage behavior that exploits it.

Bankruptcy and Resolution Procedures

It is impossible to write a financial contract that specifies every possible contingency. Instead, contracts rely on bankruptcy to determine outcomes in certain bad and unlikely states of the world. In bankruptcy, control of a firm is transferred from the shareholders, who no longer have a stake in losses because their shares are worth little, to the debtholders. It is in society's interest to develop bankruptcy procedures that maximize the post-bankruptcy value of a firm's assets. In particular, society should avoid the destruction of value that occurs with disorderly liquidation.

Disorderly liquidation of financial institutions is particularly costly. First, valuable knowledge that the institution has accumulated about its counterparties—borrowers, trading partners, and so on—can disappear as the institution loses employees and ceases to operate normally. Financial economists have found that the collapse of a bank has a material adverse impact on many of its borrowers.[13] Second, the prospect of a disorderly liquidation makes it more likely that a troubled financial institution will suffer a run by creditors who conclude they are better off claiming what money they can today, rather than waiting through protracted liquidation proceedings. Third, "fire sales" of specialized assets in a disorderly liquidation can depress prices and thereby spread problems to other holders of the asset class. Fourth, disorderly liquidation increases the uncertainty about the impact of a financial institution's failure on its counterparties and other claimholders. Because financial firms are tightly interconnected, this uncertainty can precipitate or intensify a financial crisis.[14]

In the United States, the standard bankruptcy code allows both for liquidation of a firm and the sale of its assets (Chapter 7), and for continued operation of a firm under the supervision of a bankruptcy judge who protects the firm from creditors' claims while a reorganization plan is approved (Chapter 11). These procedures appear to work well for nonfinancial corporations but not so well for financial organizations. The Chapter 11 approach of separating a firm's financial affairs from its nonfinancial business activities is infeasible when the business of the firm is financial transactions. Furthermore, many financial institutions rely heavily on short-term debt, possibly as a valuable discipline on bank executives who can rapidly change the risks their firms take. This makes financial firms vulnerable to a rapid withdrawal of short-term credit that is likely to occur before any event that would trigger bankruptcy.

We argue below that there is a need for a special resolution procedure that can be applied to large insolvent financial institutions. We also advocate regulatory changes that would push financial firms toward more resilient capital structures.

Bank Runs

Classic bank runs, in which depositors race to withdraw their funds before a bank fails, were one of the central contributors to the Great Depression. Deposit insurance, which was introduced after the Depression to counter this destructive process, made demand deposits one of the most stable forms of bank financing during the World Financial Crisis. Many financial institutions, however, suffered a modern version of bank runs.

Banks, especially those with investment banking activities, typically finance a significant fraction of their business with overnight commercial paper, repos, and other short-term instruments. In normal times, banks roll over this debt as it matures, taking new loans to pay off the old. In a crisis, however, uncertainty about whether a troubled institution would be able to pay off its creditors tomorrow causes lenders to stop extending credit today. Thus, short-term financing can lead to a run that is similar to a classic run on deposits.

Even some secured creditors participated in runs during the World Financial Crisis. Banks often use repurchase agreements to borrow money, securing the loan by giving the lender a financial asset, such as a Treasury bond, as collateral. Because they are over-collateralized, with assets worth perhaps $105 guaranteeing every $100 in loans, lenders view "repos" as a safe way to extend credit. When credit markets froze during the Crisis, however, lenders worried that retrieving collateral and selling it would be difficult, and not worth the small interest on an overnight loan. As a result, at various times during the Crisis many investment banks had difficulty rolling over even their secured loans. Even relatively healthy financial institutions were hampered by the trouble in the repo market after August 2007. As the market became more and more uncertain about the prices securities would fetch in a forced sale, these institutions found they could borrow less and less with the same collateral.[15]

Prime brokerage accounts also saw a run-like withdrawal by customers. Many large banks have prime brokerage groups that assist hedge funds and other institutional investors by providing financing, securities lending, clearing, custodial services, and operational support. In exchange, the funds pay fees and, critically, post collateral to secure their loans. With some restrictions that we explain in Chapter 10, the prime broker can then use the collateral in its own business, in some cases commingling it with the firm's own assets. During the Crisis, hedge funds monitored the financial well-being of their prime brokers and, like depositors in the Depression, fled with their collateral at the first sign of trouble. Bear Stearns, for example, had a large prime brokerage business. According to press accounts, one of the largest hedge funds that used Bear Stearns as a prime broker, Renaissance Technologies, withdrew $5 billion of cash in the week the firm failed. With such outflows, it is not surprising that Bear Stearns ran out of money even though it had more than $18 billion in cash a week earlier.

Like classic bank runs, modern bank runs are both destructive and self-fulfilling. Concern that a bank might be in trouble spurs its creditors and counterparties to withdraw or withhold their capital. As a result, even rumors of a problem may be enough to destroy a viable institution. The importance of modern bank runs during the World Financial Crisis is a recurring theme throughout the book, and we make several proposals that are intended to reduce the frequency of such events.

The Inadequacy of the Regulatory Structure

The World Financial Crisis made it clear that financial innovation had overwhelmed existing financial regulations. Notable examples include AIG's decision to sell an extremely large amount of credit default swaps on subprime debt to banks in the United States and abroad; the holding of Lehman paper by money market funds, particularly the Reserve Primary Fund; the complexity of the derivative books at Lehman and other investment banks; and the difficulty of simultaneously applying several countries' bankruptcy codes to the subsidiaries of multinational financial institutions.[16]

There is a trade-off between financial innovation and stability. Innovation can improve the financial system's ability to allocate resources to their highest valued use, but it can also reduce the stability of the system. The challenge is to develop regulations that improve stability without stifling innovation. In addition, regulation often leads to innovations designed to evade the regulations, which makes the financial system more fragile. For example, many of the special-purpose vehicles that imploded in the Crisis were created to get around capital requirements.

In many countries, the response of regulators to the World Financial Crisis was hampered by the fragmented nature of their regulatory systems. Financial regulations are typically designed to ensure the health of individual institutions rather than the financial system as a whole. In this book we argue that systemic regulation is an important function that requires a special mandate, and that the central bank is particularly well equipped to fulfill this function.

Finally, effective financial regulation requires that politicians, and ultimately the public, have an adequate understanding of the financial system. The political turmoil surrounding the Crisis suggests the importance of disseminating expert knowledge about finance to a broader audience. This is one of our motivations for writing this book.

WHAT WERE THE ORIGINS OF THE WORLD FINANCIAL CRISIS?

Like the origins of the First World War, the causes of the Crisis will be debated by scholars for many years.

Most observers agree that the strong run-up and subsequent sharp decline in the prices of stocks, houses, and other financial assets in developed countries was an important catalyst for the Crisis. There is disagreement, however, about whether this pattern in prices is the result of rational investor behavior or "irrational bubbles."

Some argue that the run-up before the Crisis was driven by investors who knowingly accepted unusually low expected returns, and they offer several possible reasons why. First, there was a surge of savings in emerging countries, driven by a combination of rapid economic growth and demographics. Perhaps because of a desire to accumulate foreign reserves in the aftermath of the Asia crisis of 1997–98, much of this wealth was invested in developed markets. Second, financial markets were unusually tranquil during 2003 to 2006. With low volatility, investors may have settled for a low risk premium. Third, influenced by fears of a Japanese-style deflation resulting from the market downturn of 2000–2001 and by a belief that they should not try to use monetary policy to counteract rising asset prices, central bankers in the United States maintained a loose monetary policy throughout the period.[17] And from this rational view of investors, the plunge in asset prices that accompanied the Crisis was caused by bad news about future cash flows, unexpected increases in the returns required by investors, or both.

Others suggest a more direct explanation. The high prices before the Crisis were driven by an irrational belief that prices would continue to rise, and the collapse of asset prices was the inevitable result of this mistake. Whatever the explanation, the sharp drop in asset prices both contributed to and was a symptom of the Crisis.

Other commentators argue that the financial system became vulnerable because many market participants assessed risks inaccurately during the period leading up to the World Financial Crisis. Consumers, banks, and investors in general underestimated the risk of house price declines, increasing the prices they were willing to pay for real estate, the credit they were willing to extend, and the valuations of banks that extended such credit. Banks put much weight on the recent past when they estimated value at risk, which led them to conclude that the level of risk was low and that there was little downside to having high leverage. Other market participants did not fully appreciate that high liquidity was suppressing volatility and that the process might reverse, with liquidity decreasing and volatility increasing.

More generally, the high level of financial innovation, driven in part by the declining cost of information technology, made it hard for risk assessment to keep pace with the evolving financial system.[18] The benign environment of the credit boom exacerbated this problem by tempting financial institutions to underinvest in risk management.

U.S. policymakers also contributed to the severity of the Crisis by pushing Fannie Mae and Freddie Mac to increase the availability of mortgage funding to borrowers with questionable ability to repay their mortgages. As a result of this pressure, both agencies relaxed their standards for the mortgages they purchased and guaranteed. The demand for homes by borrowers who qualified for mortgages because of these lower standards pushed up prices, and the default by many of them during the recession contributed to the drop in home prices.

The panic and run in the fall of 2008 remain the central distinguishing features of the World Financial Crisis. Asset prices have risen and fallen before, and the world economy has borne large financial losses many times without such a severe economic outcome. Conversely, losses from completely different underlying sources—commercial real estate or perhaps sovereign defaults—could cause a similar catastrophe if they again provoke too-big-to-fail chaos or runs.

This book does not seek to provide a complete diagnosis of the World Financial Crisis, nor does it take a stand on the relative importance of the contributing factors listed above. Rather, we believe our recommendations will help prevent or mitigate future crises even though we do not fully understand all the causes of the last one.

Carmen Reinhart and Kenneth Rogoff, among others, have pointed out that financial crises have occurred throughout the history of capitalism, and that these crises share many common patterns.[19] The lesson we draw from this is that no acceptable set of regulations can prevent market participants from making mistakes that create economic instability. Our purpose in this book is instead to suggest regulatory reforms that will make the system more stable despite the mistakes that are sure to come.

NOTES

1. For a review and analysis of the early developments in the World Financial Crisis, see "Symposium: The Early Phases of the Credit Crunch," *Journal of Economic Perspectives* 23, no. 1 (Winter 2009).

2. See Robert Battalio and Paul Schultz, "Regulatory Uncertainty and Market Liquidity: The 2008 Short Sale Ban's Impact on Equity Option Markets" (manuscript, University of Notre Dame, 2009).

3. See Zhiguo He, in Gu Khang, and Arvind Krishnamurthy, "Balance Sheet Adjustments in the 2008 Crisis" (manuscript, Kellogg Graduate School of Management, Northwestern University, and the University of Chicago Booth School of Business, 2010).

4. Practitioners typically use the term "arbitrage" to describe trades that have low risk and high expected profit. As Andrei Shleifer and Robert Vishny emphasize in "The Limits of Arbitrage," *Journal of Finance* 52 (1997): 25–55, a lack of capital can limit investors' ability to exploit such arbitrage opportunities.

5. This brief explanation ignores important complications, such as transaction costs and default risk.

6. Tommaso Mancini Griffoli and Angelo Ranaldo, "Limits to Arbitrage during the Crisis: Funding Liquidity Constraints and Covered Interest Parity" (working paper, Swiss National Bank, 2009).

7. Nicolae Garleanu and Lasse Heje Pedersen, "Margin-Based Asset Pricing and Deviations from the Law of One Price" (working paper, New York University, 2009), look at arbitrage between corporate bonds and Treasury bonds. This arbitrage uses credit default swaps to eliminate the default risk of the corporate bond so that its yield should be comparable to that of a government security. Arvind Krishnamurthy, "Debt Markets in Crisis," *Journal of Economic Perspectives* (forthcoming, 2010), describes trades using collateralized borrowing to arbitrage differences between fixed- and floating-rate investments. The arbitrage in this case uses swap contracts to convert floating interest rate payments into fixed interest rate payments. Mark Mitchell and Todd Pulvino, "Arbitrage Crashes and the Speed of Capital" (working paper, 2009), study the pricing of convertible debt securities. In this case, they do not present a genuine arbitrage trade in the sense of generating investment strategies that yield identical cash flows. Rather, they describe nearly equivalent cash flows that hedge funds normally bet will converge, and study the properties of the returns from these investment strategies. In each of these papers there are large swings in arbitrage and near-arbitrage profits in the fall of 2008.

8. Murillo Campello, John R. Graham, and Campbell R. Harvey, "The Real Effects of Financial Constraints: Evidence from a Financial Crisis," *Journal of Financial Economics* (forthcoming, 2010).

9. V. V. Chari, Lawrence Christiano, and Patrick Kehoe, "Facts and Myths about the Financial Crisis of 2008" (manuscript, University of Minnesota and Northwestern University).

10. Victoria Ivashina and David Scharfstein, "Bank Lending During the Financial Crisis of 2008," *Journal of Financial Economics* (forthcoming, 2010).

11. For a model of this effect, see Douglas W. Diamond and Raghu Rajan, "Fear of Fire Sales and the Credit Freeze" (National Bureau of Economic Research Working Paper No. 14925, 2009).

12. One classic way to produce frequent small profits and occasional large losses is to sell deep out-of-the-money put options. When a trader sells a deep out-of-the-money put, he receives a payment in exchange for a commitment to buy an asset for much less than it is currently worth. The option will almost always expire worthless and the trader will pocket the money received for selling it. Occasionally, however, the price of the asset will fall sharply and the trader will be forced to buy the asset at a large loss.

13. See, for instance, Myron B Slovin, Marie E. Sushka, and John A. Polonchek, "The Value of Bank Durability: Borrowers as Bank Stakeholders," *Journal of Finance* 48 (1993): 247–66.

14. Ben Bernanke, "Nonmonetary Effects of the Financial Crisis in the Propagation of the Great Depression," *American Economic Review* 73 (1983): 257–76, famously argued that disorderly liquidation of banks exacerbated the Great Depression. Andrei Shleifer and Robert Vishny, "Liquidation Values and Debt Capacity: A Market Equilibrium Approach," *Journal of Finance* 47, no. 4 (September 1992): 1343–66, emphasize the importance of asset fire sales. Shleifer and Vishny argue that fire sales played an important role in the Crisis in "Unstable Banking," *Journal of Financial Economics* (forthcoming, 2010), and "Asset Fire Sales and Credit Easing" (National Bureau of Economic Research Working Paper No. 15652, 2010).

15. Gary B. Gorton and Andrew Metrick develop the analogy between modern and classic bank runs in "Securitized Banking and the Run on Repo" (National Bureau of Economic Research Working Paper No. 15223, 2009) and in "Haircuts" (National Bureau of Economic Research Working Paper No. 15273, 2009).

16. Darrell Duffie, "The Failure Mechanics of Dealer Banks," *Journal of Economic Perspectives* (forthcoming, 2010), discusses the complexities surrounding bank failures in the context of the modern financial system. This paper also clarifies the mechanisms that can generate what we have called modern bank runs.

17. Ben Bernanke, "The Global Saving Glut and the U.S. Current Account Deficit," http://www.federalreserve.gov/boarddocs/speeches/2005/20050 3102/, 2005, emphasizes the role of emerging market savings. Ricardo J. Caballero, Emmanuel Farhi, and Pierre-Olivier Gourinchas, "An Equilibrium Model of Global Imbalances and Low Interest Rates," *American Economic Review* 98 (2008): 358–93, provide a formal model. John B. Taylor,

Getting Off Track: How Government Actions and Interventions Caused, Prolonged, and Worsened the Financial Crisis (Stanford, CA: Hoover Press, 2009), instead emphasizes the role of loose monetary policy. Panelists in John Y. Campbell, ed., *Asset Prices and Monetary Policy* (Chicago: University of Chicago Press, 2006), debate whether monetary policy can identify and lean against asset-price bubbles.

18. One important example is the difficulty that credit rating agencies had in extending their methodology to provide accurate assessments of the risks of securitized loan tranches. See, for example, Efraim Benmelech and Jennifer Dlugosz, "The Credit Rating Crisis," *NBER Macroeconomics Annual 2009* (Cambridge, MA: National Bureau of Economic Research, forthcoming).

19. Carmen Reinhart and Kenneth Rogoff, *This Time Is Different: Eight Centuries of Financial Folly* (Princeton, NJ: Princeton University Press, 2009).

Chapter 2

A Systemic Regulator for Financial Markets

Financial regulations in almost all countries are designed to ensure the soundness of *individual* institutions, principally commercial banks, against the risk of loss on their assets. This focus on individual firms ignores critical interactions between institutions. Attempts by individual banks to remain solvent in a crisis, for example, can undermine the stability of the system as a whole. If one financial institution prudently reduces its lending to a second, the loss of funding may cause grave problems for the borrower. We saw this in the World Financial Crisis when Bear Stearns, Lehman Brothers, and the U.K. bank Northern Rock were unable to roll over their obligations. Similarly, the failure of one financial institution can threaten the viability of many others.

The focus on individual institutions can also cause regulators to overlook important changes in the overall financial system. For example, although the markets for securitized assets and the shadow banking system of lightly regulated financial institutions grew dramatically in the years before the Crisis, the existing regulatory structures did not evolve with them.

To avoid this narrow institutional focus, *one regulatory*

organization in each country should be responsible for overseeing the health and stability of the overall financial system. The role of the systemic regulator should include gathering, analyzing, and reporting information about significant interactions and risks among financial institutions; designing and implementing systemically sensitive regulations, including capital requirements; and coordinating with the fiscal authorities and other government agencies in managing systemic crises.

We argue that the central bank should be charged with this important new responsibility. This preference is not absolute: we analyze the functions of a systemic regulator and the pros and cons of locating that regulator inside or outside the central bank. On balance, the central bank seems to be the right institution for most countries, especially those with strong, politically independent central banks that are already doing a good job managing price-level and macroeconomic stability.

WHAT SHOULD THE SYSTEMIC REGULATOR DO?

The primary role of systemic regulation should be to prevent financial crises without stifling financial innovation or long-term economic growth.

First, the systemic regulator should gather, analyze, and report systemic information. In the next chapter, we argue that a new information infrastructure is needed for regulators to understand trends and emerging risks in the financial industry. This will require a broad set of financial institutions to report standardized measures of position values and risk exposures. Such information is valueless unless it can be analyzed, and this is a natural function of the systemic regulator. In addition, to enhance general awareness of systemic issues, we argue in Chapter 3 that the systemic regulator should prepare an annual report to the legislature on the risks of the financial system.

Second, the systemic regulator should design and implement financial regulations with a systemic focus. For example, capital requirements for regulated financial institutions should depend on the systemic risk they pose. Large banks holding illiquid assets and relying heavily on short-term debt should be required to hold proportionately more capital than smaller banks with more liquid assets and more stable financing arrangements. As we describe in Chapter 5, the systemic regulator should design and administer these capital requirements, and should negotiate with regulatory authorities in other countries to ensure that capital requirements are broadly comparable internationally. The regulator should also be able to set standards for other systemically important factors, such as margins and collateral rules that influence activity in the entire financial system.

The crisis prevention role of systemic regulation is paramount. Ideally, crises should be prevented. If a crisis does erupt, however, a third role for the systemic regulator is to contribute to the management of the crisis.

We argue in Chapter 7 that banks should be encouraged, and possibly required, to issue hybrid securities that have the properties of debt unless and until a financial crisis occurs. At that time, the securities convert to equity if the financial condition of the issuing bank is sufficiently weak, recapitalizing the bank in an efficient manner without any need for an injection of taxpayer funds. The systemic regulator should be responsible for declaring the occurrence of a financial crisis, which is one part of our proposed double trigger for the conversion from debt to equity.

To be sure, the fiscal authority (for example, the Treasury and the Federal Deposit Insurance Corporation in the United States) will be responsible for the use of public funds, but the systemic regulator will be the eyes and ears of the coordinated public response once a financial crisis is under way, as well as the channel for specific policy responses such as emergency loans to mitigate the crisis.

Defining just what constitutes a "systemic" problem during a financial crisis will be a central challenge for the systemic regulator and for those crafting legislation that empowers and limits the regulator. No precise definition of a "systemic" problem exists. We do not have one and we are not aware of anyone who does. The structure of systemic regulation must therefore reflect the fact that the concept is elusive and that officials might feel a strong temptation to invoke ill-defined "systemic" fears as a pretext for unwarranted action. At a minimum, before taking a specific action the systemic regulator should be required to explain in writing the precise systemic concern that motivates that action and document that the systemic benefits are clearly greater than the short-term and long-term costs of the action. The systemic regulator should reassess these costs several years after the intervention as part of its annual report to the legislature. By providing a more accurate estimate of the costs of the intervention, this reassessment will enhance the systemic regulator's accountability.

WHY IT IS IMPORTANT TO SEPARATE SYSTEMIC REGULATION FROM OTHER FINANCIAL REGULATION

Financial regulators are often asked to protect consumers and to enforce "conduct of business" rules against insider trading and other market abuses. The skills and mindset required to fulfill these important regulatory roles are fundamentally different from those required of a systemic regulator.

Protecting consumers and prosecuting market abuse involve setting and then enforcing the appropriate rules under a transparent legal framework. Such work is primarily done by lawyers and accountants who specialize in rule-making and enforcement. As we saw with the U.S. Securities and Exchange Commission (SEC) during the World Financial Crisis, a legally oriented, rule-enforcing regulator is ill-equipped to cope with a systemic crisis caused by a financial system that has outgrown the existing set of rules. What is needed is a regulator with the expertise to monitor financial innovations, such as the growth of the shadow banking system; to diagnose likely weaknesses in the financial system; and to pursue policies that can head off likely systemic problems.

The orientation of an effective systemic regulator must be different from that of a rule-enforcing consumer protection or conduct of business regulator. A regulator charged with both enforcing rules and managing systemic risk will eventually devote too much of its attention to rule enforcement. By their nature, severe systemic crises are rare events. In the normal day-to-day business of a regulatory organization, the individuals who flourish are those who have demonstrated expertise solving current problems, not those addressing systemic concerns that may never materialize. As a result, the regulatory culture will gravitate toward consumer protection and conduct of business roles. This is apparent in the behavior of the financial regulators around the world who have adopted the U.K.-style unified regulatory system.[1]

A second problem with the combination of systemic and consumer regulation is that consumer regulation is highly charged politically. Because consumer regulation affects so many constituents, politicians sometimes put tremendous pressure on regulators to take actions to protect consumers, and do so despite potential adverse consequences. Political pressure that is applied to a systemic regulator because politicians are unhappy with its role as a consumer regulator may interfere with its independence and ability to perform systemic regulation.

The arguments above imply that the systemic regulator should not also be responsible for the regulation of business practices and consumer protection.

WHY CENTRAL BANKS SHOULD SERVE AS SYSTEMIC REGULATORS

The central bank is the natural choice to serve as the systemic regulator for four reasons.

First, the central bank has daily trading relationships with market participants as part of its core function of implementing monetary policy, and is well placed to monitor market events and to flag looming problems in the financial system. It has experience, an established sense of institutional mission, and authority with the public. No other public institution has comparable insight into and access to the broad flows in the financial system.

Second, the central bank's mandate to preserve macroeconomic stability meshes well with its role of ensuring the stability of the financial system. Macroeconomic downturns are often tightly connected to the financial system, and similar analyses, drawing on the disciplines of macroeconomics and financial economics, can provide guidance for both types of oversight. As a result, macroeconomic policy and systemic regulation are tailor-made for each other.

Third, central banks are among the most independent of government agencies.[2] Successful systemic regulation requires a focus on the long run. Because they face relatively short reelection cycles, politicians tend to focus on the short run. Insulating the systemic regulator from day-to-day interference by politicians will help ensure a systemic regulator's success. The respect and independence that central banks enjoy therefore make them natural candidates to be systemic regulators.

Fourth, the central bank is the lender of last resort. It has a balance sheet that it can use as a tool to meet systemic financial crises. As the lender of last resort, it will be called on to provide emergency funding in times of crisis. Too often during the World Financial Crisis, central banks were drawn in at the last minute to provide funding to institutions about which they had no firsthand knowledge. Northern Rock in the United Kingdom was supervised by the Financial Services Authority (FSA) and Bear Stearns in the United States was supervised by the SEC. No amount of information sharing can substitute for the firsthand information gathered in direct on-site examinations. If a central bank will be asked to lend money to save an institution once a crisis occurs, it makes sense for the central bank to gather firsthand supervisory information before the crisis.

Simply giving a central bank the authority to regulate systemic risk will not ensure that it devotes the appropriate attention and resources to the task. *Each central bank should have an explicit mandate to maintain the stability of the financial system so that it properly balances its role as a systemic regulator with its other mandates.*

Different central banks operate with different mandates. Some pursue a sole objective, such as price stability or a currency peg. Others pursue a dual mandate, such as the Federal Reserve's joint goals of price stability and maximum employment. Whatever a central bank's current charge, it should be expanded to encompass stability of the financial system.

We recognize the challenges that are introduced when a financial stability mandate is added to the duties of the central bank. The clear focus on achieving output and price stability will become blurred once the central bank also takes account of financial stability objectives. There are also legitimate concerns about the central bank overreaching itself in the resolution stage of a crisis when it greatly extends its balance sheet to lend to private institutions. Finally, we recognize the dangers of increased politicization of the central bank's actions due to its role in the resolution stage of a crisis.

However, given the importance of the financial stability goal and the fact that *some* institution must play the role of the systemic regulator, we believe that the central bank should take on the task, despite the difficulties this will pose. If another institution were responsible for systemic regulation, it would have to coordinate closely with the central bank, in a way that separate institutions are seldom able to do.

Some safeguards can mitigate the difficulties. For example, some central banks have used long-run inflation targets to keep the price stability goal firmly in view. In the resolution stage of crises, a clear demarcation of roles is important, especially when the use of public funds is contemplated. Only the fiscal authority (the Treasury and FDIC with approval from Congress in the United States, for example) can authorize the use of public funds. The central bank as the systemic regulator assists the fiscal authorities, but it is the fiscal authorities who must ultimately be responsible in any resolution effort.

Central bank independence is important for price-level stability and monetary policy, but that independence comes with limitations on the central bank's authority, typically only to lend against specific high-quality collateral. The systemic regulator must probe more deeply into specific businesses and financial markets, allocate credit to specific institutions, offer broader support, and manage the failure of large institutions. Such actions cannot be pursued with the same independence granted to monetary policy. We believe, however, that procedures for review and oversight of systemic functions of the central bank can be instituted while maintaining the independence of the central bank's monetary policy functions, and without forcing an institutional separation between the central bank and a systemic regulator.

RECOMMENDATIONS

RECOMMENDATION 1. *The regulatory structure for financial markets and institutions should include a systemic regulator that oversees the health and stability of the overall financial system.* A systemic regulator will be able to limit systemic shocks of the sort that have recently arisen from the shadow banking system and from spillovers between financial institutions.

RECOMMENDATION 2. *The central bank should be the systemic financial regulator.* Central banks' independence, daily interactions with the markets, focus on macroeconomic stability, and role as lenders of last resort make them the natural systemic regulators.

RECOMMENDATION 3. *The systemic regulator (the central bank) should not also be responsible for the regulation of business practices and consumer protection. Those roles should be given to one or more separate agencies.* The systemic regulator will be better able to maintain the proper organizational culture and resist political pressure if it is not burdened with these responsibilities.

RECOMMENDATION 4. *The systemic regulator (the central bank) must be given adequate resources.* Without sufficient resources, the systemic regulator will not be able to identify systemic risks and craft the needed regulations to promote financial stability. During the World Financial Crisis, the staff of central banks like the Federal Reserve was stretched to the limit. Asking central banks to become systemic regulators will stretch already thin resources even thinner, perhaps even compromising the banks' ability to conduct monetary policy successfully.

RECOMMENDATION 5. *The central bank should be given an explicit mandate for maintaining the systemic stability of the financial system.* This will ensure that the central bank properly balances its role as systemic regulator with its other mandates. The goals for central banks should be expanded to include financial stability.

NOTES

1. This is an example of the general human tendency, emphasized by a string of observers from Howard Kunreuther to Richard Posner, to spend too little time and effort preparing contingency plans to handle rare catastrophic events.
2. There has been increasing recognition in recent decades that central banks have an important stabilizing role to play and as such should be independent of short-run political pressures. Many countries have adopted laws to ensure this independence. See Alan Blinder, *The Quiet Revolution: Central Banking Goes Modern* (New Haven, CT: Yale University Press, 2004).

Chapter 3

A New Information Infrastructure for Financial Markets

Information about prices and quantities of assets lies at the heart of well-functioning capital markets. During the World Financial Crisis, it became apparent that many important actors—both firms and regulatory agencies—did not have sufficient information. In this chapter we propose a new regulatory regime for gathering and disseminating financial market information. We argue that government regulators need a new infrastructure to collect and analyze adequate information from systemically important financial institutions. Our new information framework would bolster the government's ability to foresee, contain, and ideally prevent disruptions to the overall financial services industry. We also suggest that the information reported to regulators should be available to the general public with a time lag. This will enhance the market's ability to regulate itself.

WHY INFORMATION IS CRITICAL, AND WHAT INFORMATION GAPS CURRENTLY EXIST

Much of the information regulators currently collect from U.S. financial institutions focuses on the health and potential failure of each institution individually. Regulators collect far less information about the systemic interactions between institutions. The failure of one bank, for example, might have little impact on other firms, while the failure of another bank might have a devastating impact on the whole financial system. Knowledge of such differences is important for effective regulation of the financial system.

Each financial institution is vulnerable to institution-specific risks, such as the performance of its particular assets and the quality of its management. But financial institutions also face two important forms of systemic risk. *Counterparty risk* (described further in Chapter 9) arises when one institution owes money to a trading partner, perhaps because the partner has unrealized gains on the contracts that link the firms. The trading partner has counterparty risk because it will suffer losses if the other firm defaults.

Fire-sale risk is a bit more complicated. Firms often push security prices down when they sell large positions. Part of the price drop is permanent and is attributable to (1) any information revealed by the firm's decision to sell at the current price and (2) the fact that others must now absorb the risk formerly borne by the firm. Fire-sale risk arises because the price drop also has a second, temporary component. If the firm tries to sell a large position quickly, it must offer a price concession to attract the limited number of buyers who are currently in the market. The size of the temporary price concession depends on how much is being sold, how quickly the firm wants to sell, and how many buyers are available and ready to trade.[1]

The temporary part of the price drop can have real effects despite its transitory nature. For example, the temporary price concession reduces the amount a firm receives if it must sell large positions quickly to reduce its risk. The temporary component can also affect firms that do not initially sell at the fire-sale price. For example, the low market price may cause creditors to demand more collateral, or the firms may suffer a reduction in regulatory capital if they are forced to mark their assets to the market price.

Fire-sale risk can be systemic. First, the magnitude of the temporary component of the price drop depends on how much is being sold. Thus, if many firms rush to the exit simultaneously, the price concession can be especially large. Second, because of mark to market accounting, fire sales by some firms may force others to liquidate positions to satisfy capital requirements. These successive sales can magnify the original temporary price drop and force more sales.

Because of counterparty and fire-sale risk, an otherwise sound firm can be dragged down by the failure of others. As the insurer and lender of last resort for banks and many other financial institutions, the government needs sufficient information to monitor these risks. We believe that the government should collect information from all systemically important institutions, including both heavily regulated institutions, such as large commercial banks, and less regulated institutions, such as hedge funds.

To monitor systemic risk, the government needs information about two broad categories of financial instruments:

1. *Derivative positions*, such as forward contracts, swaps, and options. Since a firm's payoff on these contracts depends on the performance of a clearinghouse or trading partner, they contribute to *counterparty risk*. This information should be detailed enough to allow regulators to identify significant counterparties shared by many systemically important institutions, such as Lehman Brothers and AIG during the World Financial Crisis.
2. *More general asset positions*, such as bonds, mortgages, and asset backed securities. Together with the information about derivative positions, regulators can combine this information across institutions to identify large aggregate positions that create systemic fire-sale risk. Recent examples of large common holdings include collateralized mortgage obligations and securitized credit card debt.

What specific information is needed about these positions? A starting point is the current valuation of a firm's positions, but this is not enough by itself. The government also needs to be able to assess the risk exposures of the firm's positions, which are the sensitivities of their values to changes in market conditions. This is particularly important for derivative positions, which are often structured so that cash transfers between counterparties keep current values at or close to zero but which can create large gains or losses as market conditions change.

The importance of linking this information across institutions is obvious. Regulators cannot assess the status of the financial system without knowledge of the interactions between firms. *Currently, U.S. regulators do not systematically gather and analyze much of the information outlined above, and the information they do have is often difficult or impossible to aggregate across institutions. This constrains the government's ability to foresee, contain, and, ideally, prevent disruptions to the overall financial services industry.* The September 2008 failure of AIG is a good example. It is now clear that few if any regulators understood AIG's outsized credit default swap positions until AIG itself approached regulators under great duress.

RECOMMENDATIONS

Currently, different government regulators do collect some information from financial institutions, such as the quarterly 10Q accounting statements U.S. firms must file with the SEC and the Reports of Condition and Income U.S. banks must file with the Federal Reserve. But this information does not cover the full set outlined above. *Government regulators need new authority and a new infrastructure to collect and analyze adequate information from all finan-*

cial institutions. This new information regime should be structured with five main features.

RECOMMENDATION 1. *All large financial institutions should report information about asset positions and risks to regulators each quarter.* Quarterly disclosure will balance timeliness against reporting burden. "Window dressing," in which an institution alters its exposures at quarter end to mask its typical risk, is a potential problem. But we do not think it will undermine the usefulness of our proposed regime, and its incidence will be curbed by the cost of temporarily shifting positions.

We stress that in this new framework, greater information would be collected from some institutions that currently face limited oversight, such as hedge funds. We are sensitive to the potential burden a reporting requirement such as this can create for these firms. Nevertheless, as the hedge fund Long-Term Capital Management demonstrated vividly in 1998, these institutions can have systemic effects.

More generally, one of the benefits of broader information disclosure could be to force more companies to generate and aggregate this information themselves. This could foster better internal risk management in firms, something that seemed acutely lacking in many companies in the run-up to the World Financial Crisis.

RECOMMENDATION 2. *To maximize the value of information collected, regulators need to standardize the process used to measure valuations and risk exposures.* Where they are available, firms should report the current market values of their asset and derivatives positions. Market values should also be used as inputs when firms calculate their risk exposures. When model-based valuations are used for hard-to-value assets, regulators should enforce some consistency across institutions. One possibility is for each firm to value its positions using a standard set of models. Regulators should also develop a standard set of factors (such as movements in short-term and long-term interest rates, domestic and foreign stock returns, real estate prices, and foreign currencies) that institutions should use to assess their risks. Firms could then report the dollar amount of their gains and losses from specific changes in these factors, both for the assets they own and for their derivative positions. The asset values and risk sensitivities should be reported for standardized asset classes, and the sensitivities for derivative positions should be broken down by counterparty. Of course, the asset classes and standard factors must be redefined periodically as market conditions change.

Although we advocate the use of market values wherever possible in value and risk reporting, we are not arguing for or against using market values for other purposes, such as mark to market accounting or the calculation of regulatory capital for commercial banks. It is clear that the advantages of market valuations outweigh the disadvantages when measuring systemic risks, but the more general use of market values is a separate issue that we do not address.

RECOMMENDATION 3. *To foster sound analysis of the information collected, different regulatory agencies need authority* *to share information.* We see at least two distinct merits in widespread information sharing across agencies. One is to allow each agency to better conduct its specific functions. The other is to foster among all agencies greater awareness of systemic patterns.

RECOMMENDATION 4. *After some time lag the information collected by regulators each quarter should be released to the private sector.* Regulatory capacity is limited: despite talented individuals with good intentions throughout regulatory agencies, the inherent complexity of financial markets means potential problems can be difficult to recognize and respond to. Given this, there is high value in complementing government analysis of financial system information with that of private actors.

That said, it is important to protect proprietary business models and incentives to innovate. Public disclosure of a firm's positions also raises concerns about predatory or copycat trading by competitors. To mitigate these problems, public disclosure will be delayed and the length of this delay will depend on the extent to which information is aggregated. For example, industry-wide exposures should be released soon after the information is collected, while exposures for individual firms may be withheld for three, six, or even twelve months.

RECOMMENDATION 5. *To elevate the importance of financial system information, the systemic regulator should prepare an annual "risk of the financial system" report for the legislature.* The report could summarize how asset positions, fire-sale exposures, and counterparty exposures for various parts of a country's financial system evolved during the year. It will add value both directly, through its contents, and indirectly, by fostering a higher public profile for sound regulation of capital markets.

CONCLUSION

The new information infrastructure for capital markets that we have outlined in this chapter would likely need new legislation to be integrated into the existing procedures used by financial market regulators such as the Federal Reserve, the Federal Deposit Insurance Corporation, the SEC, the Commodities and Futures Trading Commission, and the designated systemic regulator. Guidance about the best way to create this infrastructure in a particular country would be needed from heads of the relevant agencies in that country.

NOTE

1. Andrei Shleifer and Robert Vishny, "Liquidation Values and Debt Capacity: A Market Equilibrium Approach," *Journal of Finance* 47, no. 4 (September 1992): 1343–66.

Chapter 4

Regulation of Retirement Savings

Retirement saving is undergoing a fundamental change as employers shift from defined benefit pension plans to defined contribution plans, such as 401(k) accounts. Defined contribution plans have important advantages: they allow households to customize their retirement saving to their own risk preferences and circumstances, they insulate pensioners from potential bankruptcies of their employers, and, although there may be a modest vesting period, they allow workers to move from job to job without risking their pensions.

These plans also place much greater burdens on consumers to make good financial decisions. There is widespread concern that many households are not up to the task. In this chapter, we analyze this concern and recommend measures that will improve the performance of the nation's retirement saving system. Our discussion and recommendations are oriented toward U.S. defined contribution plans, which are offered by most American companies, but the concepts we develop are applicable around the world.

We recommend changes in disclosure requirements and investment options. To be eligible for defined contribution plan investments, a mutual fund should be required to provide a simple, standardized disclosure of the costs and risks of investing in the fund. Our model is the nutrition label required for packaged foods in the United States. The investment label should emphasize tangible characteristics that are related to cost and risk. Expense ratios, for example, should be prominent.

When trying to forecast future investment returns, investors often overestimate the information in prior returns. Even five-year return histories are of almost no use in forecasting future relative performance. For this reason, we recommend that the standardized disclosure should not include information about prior returns. To help investors understand the limited value of prior returns, sponsors of investment products for defined contribution plans who report their average prior return in advertising or other disclosures should be required to report a standardized measure of the uncertainty associated with the average.

We also advocate improved default options for defined contribution plans. If employees do not select an alternative, they should be automatically enrolled in their employer's defined contribution plan. Many participants in defined contribution plans tend to anchor their investment decisions on the default options, as though those were optimal. To increase the amount employees save for retirement, we recommend an aggressive default withholding rate that increases over time. The default investment should be well diversified and have low fees.

Finally, there should be more restrictions on the investments employees can include in their defined contribution plans. There should be strict limits, for example, on investments in the stock of one's employer.

Our standardized disclosure is not meant to replace the standard investment prospectus, or even the SEC's new summary prospectus. Our goal is to communicate tangible and easily understood measures of cost and risk that can have first-order effects on an employee's investment experience. The uniform format of the disclosure label will facilitate comparisons across investments and help employees develop perspective as they compare alternatives over time. It is tempting to recommend the inclusion of many other measures that we know are important, but doing so would defeat the purpose of the label; few employees read required disclosures that are long and complicated, just as few home buyers study the many pages of disclosures in their mortgage contracts before pledging to make years of payments. Motivated employees who want more detail can always find it in the prospectus and the statement of additional information.

Our recommendations about default options build on provisions of the Pension Protection Act of 2006. The Act gives employers the option to automatically enroll employees who do not explicitly opt out of defined contribution plans. We argue that automatic enrollment should be the default option for all defined contribution plans. The default withholding rates we recommend are also more aggressive than the safe harbor rates in the Pension Protection Act.

THE NEED FOR REGULATION OF
RETIREMENT SAVING

A large body of research has found that many people make costly mistakes in retirement planning. They do not save enough, so their standard of living falls substantially on retirement. They hold insufficiently diversified portfolios, exposing themselves to needless risk. Many invest much of their retirement savings in company stock, which means that if their company fails, their savings disappear at the same time that they lose their jobs. Others hold high-fee funds that on average deliver poor long-term performance. Some change their allocations far too often, while many others never revisit an allocation made on the first day of the job.[1]

There are several reasons why it is appropriate for public policy to help reduce such mistakes. First, people who reach old age with inadequate financial resources become eligible for public assistance, such as Medicaid. Taxpayers have a legitimate interest in preventing this outcome. It is also likely that, if many people lose substantial sums in their retirement accounts, there will be great pressure for the government to provide additional financial support.

Second, the possibility of social assistance creates what economists call moral hazard: people are less likely to save or to properly consider the downside risks of their investment decisions if the government will support retirees who cannot support themselves. Provision of aid to the unfortunate should be accompanied by pressure not to become unfortunate in the first place.

Third, it is difficult to make wise decisions about retirement savings and investment. The mistakes people make about their retirement savings have been attributed to financial illiteracy and to a number of psychological biases: misperception of risks; procrastination; inadequate self-discipline; inertia; and overconfidence, which leads most active investors to the illogical conclusion that each can outsmart the others. Learning to invest well is difficult, and to the extent that the government can help people make good decisions—an important caveat—it can improve welfare by doing so.

Of course, the fact that people make poor decisions does not, by itself, justify regulation. Regulation is a blunt instrument. It has costs and unintended consequences, even when implemented as intended, and the costs and unintended consequences tend to be magnified by real-world political pressures.

What are the costs? First, rules intended to protect consumers in financial markets can end up simply excluding poor and less creditworthy people from the benefits of financial market participation. Second, even apparently benign disclosure rules can create the unhealthy expectation that the government is responsible for identifying the risks people might encounter in life. Third, the disclosure and regulatory process can be captured by industry.

Finally, we note that government policy itself has contributed to the problem of inadequate retirement saving. One prominent reason for low savings rates in the United States is the high taxation of savings. Tax-advantaged defined contribution plans, such as individual retirement accounts and 401(k) plans, reduce but do not eliminate the problem. A general overhaul of the U.S. tax code to address this issue is far beyond the scope of our book. Instead, we take the current tax code as a given and offer suggestions to make defined contribution plans more effective.

Because the benefits from the regulation of retirement saving must be balanced against the potential costs, we recommend relatively mild regulations that are less open to capture and other unintended consequences. We do not advocate more aggressive policies, such as a legislated move away from defined contribution back toward defined benefit plans, severe limitations on eligible investments, or government takeover of pensions.

RECOMMENDATIONS

Our recommendations fall into two groups. The first five concern disclosure and the last three concern permissible investment options.

RECOMMENDATION 1. *Investment products offered to defined contribution plans should include a simple standardized disclosure label to encourage comparison shopping on important attributes. Although we offer some recommendations about what should and should not be on the label, the form and technical specifications should be developed by a committee of academics, regulators, and industry experts.* Our model is the nutrition label on food products.

The standardized disclosure label should emphasize tangible characteristics that will provide meaningful information about the cost and risk of the investment. It will be tempting to include a wide range of information that a motivated employee might consider when comparing investment alternatives. These details, however, will continue to be available in the investment prospectus and the statement of additional information. The standardized disclosure label is a tool to help employees who are less motivated or less prepared to make better investment choices. The appendix to this chapter offers an example of the label for a generic S&P 500 index fund.

RECOMMENDATION 2. *Investment costs, including the expense ratio (annual cost), front-end load (initial cost), and back-end load (final cost), should be prominent in the standardized disclosure label.* Fees above a threshold should trigger a warning about the long-term consequences of high fees, analogous to the surgeon general's warning on a package of cigarettes. High-fee funds argue that their fees are justified by superior performance. A large body of academic research challenges that argument. On average, high fees are simply a net drain to investors. While some investors might gain by selecting successful high-fee funds, the negative-sum nature of the process implies that other investors must lose even more. Most employees saving for retirement are poorly placed to compete in this game. They should not be forbidden from doing so, but disclosure of high fees and a "surgeon general's warning" are appropriate.

High turnover is also a drag on average returns because it creates high transaction costs. Some funds may be able to profit at the expense of others by high turnover, but again, identifying future winners is very difficult. Turnover should also be included in disclosure for this reason.

RECOMMENDATION 3. *The standardized disclosure should present simple but meaningful measures of long-term risk.* Our analysis suggests the label should report two complementary measures. The first is the annualized volatility of the inflation-adjusted ten-year return. The other is the range of inflation-adjusted payoffs a $1,000 investment might produce in ten years, including the average and the fifth, fiftieth, and ninety-fifth percentiles.

It is not a trivial task to calculate these measures of long-term risk correctly. One important difficulty is that the relation between short-term and long-term volatility varies across investments. Stock returns are roughly independent through time; a high return this year does not imply much about the return next year. In contrast, the annual real returns on Treasury Inflation Protected Securities (TIPS) are mean-reverting; a high annual real return on two-year TIPS, for example, must be followed by an offsetting low return. Thus, although the variance of the payoff on a stock portfolio grows roughly linearly with time, the variance of the payoff on a fixed income portfolio grows less quickly (and may even decline). For this reason we recommend that standardized procedures for calculating long-term risk should be developed by a committee of experts on financial market returns and asset allocation.[2]

RECOMMENDATION 4. *Past returns should not be reported in the standardized disclosure label.* A large body of research finds that past returns in general, and short-term returns in particular, are almost useless in forecasting subsequent investment performance. We expect that some vendors of investment products will push hard to include past returns in the standardized disclosure label. The label, however, is intended to warn of the costs and risks of investments, not to help firms market their products.

RECOMMENDATION 5. *Whenever an advertisement or other disclosure about an investment product offered to defined contribution plans reports an average prior return, it must also include a standardized measure of the uncertainty associated with the average.* Our goal is not to provide a precise statistical statement about future expected returns, but rather to give investors perspective about what an average prior return implies about the future. For example, sponsors of investment products might be required to report the "margin of error," which we define as twice the standard error of the average return, whenever they report an average prior return. Speaking loosely, the difference between the historical average and the true expected return during the prior period is within the margin of error about 95 percent of the time.[3]

While improved disclosure is important, it is not sufficient. There is considerable evidence that outcomes can be improved by offering savers suitable default investment options that will apply unless they actively opt out by making a different decision.[4]

The default options for defined contribution plans should encourage an aggressive savings rate and should nudge employees toward low-fee, diversified investments. In our recommendations, we split defined contribution savings into a standard account and a supplemental account. The supplemental account is accumulated through investments made with savings in excess of perhaps 10 percent of compensation each year, plus any employer match on this part of the employee's savings. The standard account is accumulated through savings below 10 percent of annual compensation, plus employer contributions not specifically linked to savings in excess of 10 percent of compensation. Although employees should face only limited restrictions when investing the supplemental portion of their defined contribution savings, investment choices for the standard portion should be more constrained.

Recommendation 6. *Eligible employees who do not explicitly opt out should be automatically enrolled in their firm's defined contribution plan, and the default savings rate should be a substantial portion of the employee's compensation. For example, the default withholding rate (the fraction of annual compensation withheld) might start at 5 percent in the first year, then grow by 0.5 percent per year to a maximum of 10 percent (subject to IRS limits). The default investment should be a portfolio of low-fee, diversified products.* Many employees select the default options when they enroll in a defined contribution plan and others anchor their choices on the default options. A high default contribution rate will increase the retirement savings of those employees. Academic research provides compelling evidence that higher fees and expenses reduce the returns to investors. Thus, default investments should include only low-fee, diversified products.

RECOMMENDATION 7. *The standard part of an employee's defined contribution savings should be invested only in diversified products, and the fees on these products should not be excessive.* Investments in the standard account should be restricted to well-diversified products with annual fees below a specific limit.

RECOMMENDATION 8. *There should be strict limits on the amount of their own company's stock employees can hold in the standard part of their defined contribution accounts.* Although compensation linked to equity can be a useful tool for aligning the interests of management and shareholders, employees should not hold their retirement savings in their employer's stock. First, a concentrated position in any company creates unnecessary investment risk. Second, and probably more important, employees who invest in their employer's stock may lose both their pension and their job if their employer falls on hard times. Company stock may be included in a diversified investment product held in an employee's standard retirement account, but only as an "incidental" result of the investment manager's overall strategy.

APPENDIX: STANDARDIZED DISCLOSURE LABEL

Fund Name   Classic Market Index
Fund Type   U.S. Equity

	Annual	Buy	Sell	10-Year
Fees and Expenses	0.30%	0.00%	0.00%	4.67%

	5%	50%	Average	95%
Possible 10-Year Payoffs (per $100)	$49.54	$132.27	$158.07	$353.16

Turnover	4.00%			
Annual Volatility	20.00%			

Fees and Expenses and **Possible Payoffs** assume that, after making an initial investment, you reinvest all distributions and then sell the fund in ten years.

Fees and Expenses

Annual   The percentage of your fund holdings that you pay for fees and expenses each year.

Buy   The percentage of your investment that the manager takes when you buy this fund.

Sell   The percentage of your fund holdings that the manager takes when you sell this fund.

10-Year   The percentage of your investment that you will pay for fees and expenses (including buy and sell charges), on average, if you invest for ten years.

Possible 10-Year Payoffs

If you invest $100 for ten years, the final (inflation-adjusted) value of your savings will be below the **5 percent** payoff roughly 5 percent of the time, below the **50 percent** payoff roughly half the time, and below the **95 percent** payoff roughly 95 percent of the time. Payoffs that are even more extreme than the 5 percent and 95 percent payoffs are possible. **Average** is the average of all possible payoffs.

Turnover   The percentage of the investment portfolio bought and sold each year.

Annual Volatility   A measure of risk. In a typical year, the return will fluctuate up or down by this much.

NOTES

1. Recent papers presenting evidence of investment mistakes in retirement saving include Sumit Agarwal, John C. Driscoll, Xavier Gabaix, and David Laibson, "The Age of Reason: Financial Decisions over the Life Cycle and Implications for Regulation," *Brookings Papers on Economic Activity* (Fall 2009), and James J. Choi, David Laibson, and Brigitte C. Madrian, "$100 Bills on the Sidewalk: Suboptimal Investment in 401(k) Plans" (unpublished working paper, Yale University and Harvard University, 2009). John Y. Campbell, "Household Finance," *Journal of Finance* 61 (2006): 1553–1604, provides a general survey of household investment mistakes.

2. One promising approach to this problem starts by allocating securities to five asset classes: stock, cash (such as money market accounts), Treasury bonds, corporate bonds, and inflation-protected securities. We then split the return on each investment into the return on its asset class (or mix of asset classes) and an investment-specific component. We assume any mean reversion happens at the asset-class level. Thus, an investment's ten-year variance is the historical ten-year variance of its asset class (or mix of asset classes) plus ten times the annual variance of its investment-specific return. This simple approach ignores issues that might be important in other applications, such as risk management, but it offers a standardized and robust way to compare long-term investments. Finally, to prevent employees from drawing inappropriate inferences from past returns, when calculating the range of ten-year outcomes we would use the same expected return for all investments in a particular asset class. For example, the calculations might assume the expected real return on all stocks is 5 percent.

3. For example, the long-term standard deviation on the U.S. stock market is around 20 percent per year. If a mutual fund invested in U.S. stocks has the same 20 percent volatility, the margin of error is 40 percent for the

one-year average return, 17.9 percent for the five-year average, and 12.6 percent for the ten-year average return. Again speaking loosely, if the true expected return is 10 percent, the one-year average return will be between –30 percent and 50 percent, the five-year average return will be between –7.9 percent and 27.9 percent, and the ten-year average return will be between –2.6 percent and 22.6 percent about 95 percent of the time. These calculations are based on the standard formula that assumes returns are independently distributed in successive years. Margins of error for the difference between a fund and market performance are typically smaller, and can be reported when a fund chooses to report that difference.

4. See, for example, Brigitte C. Madrian and Dennis F. Shea, "The Power of Suggestion: Inertia in 401(k) Participation and Savings Behavior," *Quarterly Journal of Economics* 116 (2001): 1149–87. Richard Thaler and Cass Sunstein, *Nudge: Improving Decisions About Health, Wealth, and Happiness* (New Haven, CT: Yale University Press, 2008), argue for broader use of default options to improve economic and social outcomes.

Chapter 5

Reforming Capital Requirements

Banks help allocate society's limited savings to the most productive investments, and they facilitate the efficient sharing of the risks of those investments. As the World Financial Crisis forcefully reminded us, a breakdown in this process can disrupt economies around the world. Because other financial institutions can step in to fill the gap, the failure of an isolated bank is unlikely to cause serious economy-wide problems. Large banks, however, are rarely isolated. Many are linked through complex webs of trading relationships, so the failure of one large bank can inflict significant losses on others.

The contamination across institutions is not limited to defaults. A bank that simply suffers large losses may be forced to reduce its risk by selling assets at distressed or fire-sale prices. If other banks must revalue their assets at these temporarily low market values, the first sale can set off a cascade of fire sales that inflicts losses on many institutions. Thus, whether through default or fire sales, one troubled bank can damage many others, reducing the financial system's capacity to bear risk and make loans.

Banks in the United States and many other countries must

satisfy regulatory capital requirements that are intended to ensure they can sustain reasonable losses. These requirements are generally specified as a ratio of some measure of capital to some measure of assets, such as total assets or risk-adjusted assets. Capital requirements are typically designed as if each bank were an isolated entity, with little concern for the effect losses or default at one bank can have on other financial institutions. We argue that regulators should recognize these systemic effects when setting capital requirements. The failure of a large national bank, for example, is almost certain to have a bigger impact on the banking system and the wider economy than the failure of several small regional banks that together do the same amount of business as the large bank. Thus, if everything else is the same, large banks should face higher capital requirements than small banks.

Similarly, because the process of frequently going to the market for external financing provides valuable discipline on management, banks find it cheaper to finance much of their operations with short-term debt. Short-term financing, however, can create problems. In a crisis, banks may not be able to roll over short-term loans, perhaps because the value of their collateral has become too uncertain or because those who might provide the next round of financing fear a subsequent run. Unable to obtain short-term financing, they may be forced to sell assets at fire-sale prices and reduce the number of loans they issue. Because of these adverse systemic effects, capital requirements should be higher for banks that finance more of their operations with short-term debt.

Capital requirements are not free. The disciplining effect of short-term debt, for example, makes management more productive. Capital requirements that lean against short-term debt push banks toward other forms of financing that may allow managers to be more lax. Similarly, some large banks may capture important economies of scale that reduce the cost of financial services. When designing capital requirements that address systemic concerns, regulators must weigh the costs such requirements impose on banks during good times against the benefit of having more capital in the financial system when a crisis strikes.

Capital requirements can also affect the competitiveness of a country's banking sector. If capital requirements in the United States, for example, are too onerous, firms may turn to banks in other countries for financial services. This would undermine an important American industry. Perhaps more significant, if American firms move their banking relationships to less well capitalized financial institutions outside the United States, the U.S. government may be forced to bail out foreign banks to protect our economy in the next financial crisis. Finally, capital requirements that are too onerous may lead to a migration of activities from banks to other, less regulated financial institutions either in the United States or offshore, making it harder to identify and control systemic risks to the financial system.[1]

BANK INCENTIVES TO RAISE ADDED CAPITAL

Many banks suffered substantial losses in the World Financial Crisis, often because of a decline in the value of the mortgage backed securities they held. Each dollar of losses reduced the bank's capital by a dollar, and as a result, many banks no longer had enough capital to meet their statutory capital requirements. A bank can address this problem by reducing its liabilities or increasing its capital. During the Crisis, most banks chose to delever by making fewer new loans.

Why not simply replenish their capital by issuing equity? One important reason is related to what economists call the debt overhang problem. If a troubled bank issues equity, the new capital increases the likelihood that bondholders will be repaid and that deposit insurance will not be used. Thus, much of the new capital is captured by the bank's bondholders and by the insurer of the bank's deposits. Existing shareholders, on the other hand, bear costs because their claims on the firm are diluted. Thus, as we saw during the Crisis, shareholders often prefer that the bank satisfy its capital requirements by reducing the amount it lends. Unfortunately, the whole economy suffers when the banking sector delevers by lending less.

RECOMMENDATIONS

Banks that hold riskier assets typically have higher capital requirements. We argue that capital requirements should also vary with other characteristics that are linked to the *systemic* problems a bank might create.

RECOMMENDATION 1. *If everything else is the same, capital requirements, as a fraction of either total assets or risk-adjusted assets, should be higher for large banks.*

If losses force a large bank to sell assets at fire-sale prices, the positions it sells are likely to be bigger than those of a similarly afflicted small bank. Thus, the large bank is likely to have a bigger adverse effect on prices and on the market value of other banks' assets. Similarly, when a large bank does not have enough capital to survive its losses in a downturn, many other banks may be among the creditors who suffer. In either case, diversification—spreading the initial positions among several small banks rather than one big bank—reduces systemic problems.

Consider default by a large bank. When it fails, the bank is likely to impose large losses on a relatively small number of counterparties, and the losses will occur simultaneously. If the same losing positions are held by several small banks rather than one large bank, some may survive and spare their creditors entirely. Even if none survive, the small bank failures will probably be scattered through time. Fragile firms will fail quickly, while others will be able to sustain larger losses before failing. This will give the financial sector and regulators more time to absorb the blow. Finally, a group of small banks is likely to have a wider range of counterparties than one large firm, so their defaults will be spread over a larger capital base.

In short, potential systemic problems are bigger if the same risky positions are aggregated in one large bank rather than spread among several small banks, so capital requirements should be more than proportionately higher for large banks.

RECOMMENDATION 2: *Capital requirements should depend on the liquidity of the assets held by a bank.*

When a bank sells a large asset position quickly, its impact on price depends on the liquidity of the asset. It can sell a huge Treasury bill position with essentially no impact on price, but the quick sale of asset backed securities may require a large price concession. Such price concessions can cause systemic problems, so banks that hold less liquid assets should have higher capital requirements.

RECOMMENDATION 3. *Capital requirements for a financial institution should increase with the proportion of its debt that is short-term.*

Agency problems occur when the incentives facing a company's managers encourage them to take actions that are not in the best interests of the company's shareholders. These actions could be as simple as buying executive jets that are not really needed or as sweeping as following a corporate strategy that is excessively risky. Agency problems can be especially severe in the financial services industry. For example, banks can choose from a huge range of assets and projects to invest in, from perfectly transparent and highly liquid Treasury bills to opaque and illiquid private loans or specialized over-the-counter securities. Banks add value due to specialized skill in selecting and monitoring these illiquid assets. However, a bank's managers have an incentive to select the sorts of assets that increase their expected compensation, often at the cost of increasing the bank's risk. The managers also have an incentive to entrench themselves by selecting excessively illiquid investments that require their special expertise to manage. It is difficult for the bank's stockholders or its board of directors to control this conflict directly because the managers have much more information about the bank's investment opportunities and the projects they select. Short-term debt can reduce these agency problems. If a bank has a significant amount of short-term debt in its capital structure, it must continuously raise new funding to repay the current creditors. This forces the company and its managers to meet a continual market test, so managers have less opportunity to enrich themselves at the expense of the bank's owners.

Short-term debt provides valuable discipline inside financial firms, but it can also create systemic problems. Specifically, the need to repay the debt may force banks to dump assets and reduce lending during a financial crisis. And because each bears only a tiny slice of the systemic costs it creates, banks issue more than the socially optimal amount of short-term debt. Moreover, this systemic cost is in addition to concerns one might have about the mismatch between the maturities of a bank's assets and liabilities. Whether the bank's assets mature in two years or twenty, the risk that it will be forced to sell illiquid assets in a financial crisis increases with its use of short-term debt. Thus, it is not sufficient to make capital requirements increase in relation to the maturity mismatch between assets and liabilities.

CONCLUSION

Regulators should consider systemic effects when setting bank capital requirements. Everything else the same, capital requirements should be higher for larger banks, banks that hold more illiquid assets, and banks that finance more of their operations with short-term debt. Because they bear all the costs and receive only a small part of the societal benefits, we anticipate that banks will object to this proposal, even if regulators make the right trade-off between the costs and benefits. These complaints should not persuade regulators to forgo the benefits from systemically sensitive capital requirements.

NOTE

1. Improved capital requirements are only one of several ways to reduce the systemic risks created by financial institutions. In Chapter 7 we argue that regulators should support a new hybrid security that will expedite the recapitalization of distressed banks.

Chapter 6

Regulation of Executive Compensation in Financial Services

Many people argue that inappropriate compensation policies in financial companies contributed to the World Financial Crisis. Some say the overall *level* of pay was too high. Others criticize the *structure* of pay, claiming that contracts for CEOs, traders, and other key professionals induced them to pursue excessively risky and short-term strategies.

In this chapter, we first argue that governments should generally not regulate the *level* of executive compensation in financial institutions.[1] We have seen no convincing evidence that high levels of compensation in financial companies are inherently risky for the companies themselves or the overall economy. Moreover, limits on pay are likely to cause unintended consequences. As a result, society is better off if compensation levels are set by market forces.

The *structure* of executive compensation, however, can affect the risk of systemically important financial institutions. Robust financial institutions promote economic growth and employment. As we saw in the Crisis, this often causes governments to intervene when their financial systems are threatened. The result is privatized gains and socialized losses. If things go well, banks' owners and employees claim the profits, but if things go poorly, society subsidizes the losses. Because the owners and employees of financial firms do not bear the full cost of their failures, they have an incentive to take more risk than they otherwise would. This in turn increases the chance of bank failures, systemic risk, and taxpayer costs.

The link between the risks financial institutions take and the costs they impose on taxpayers gives society a stake in the structure of executive compensation at systemically important financial firms. To reduce employees' incentives to take excessive risk, we advocate a rule that requires systemically important financial firms to hold back a significant share of each senior manager's annual compensation for several years. Employees would forfeit their deferred compensation if their firm goes bankrupt or receives extraordinary government assistance.

GOVERNMENTS SHOULD NOT REGULATE THE LEVEL OF EXECUTIVE COMPENSATION

The World Financial Crisis has focused attention on highly compensated executives in the financial services industry. Many earn more than $10 million a year and are among the highest-paid employees in any industry.

Striking though they are, we are not convinced these high levels of compensation are inherently destabilizing to individual firms or to the overall financial system. They also are not obvious evidence of a failure of corporate governance, despite claims to the contrary. Rather, the extraordinary compensation commanded by some finance professionals can arise for a few straightforward but powerful reasons.

First, even among those with similar professional qualifications, there are tangible differences in the skills of financial employees, and even a small difference in skill can have an enormous impact on the profits of a financial firm. An extra 1 percent return on a $10 billion investment portfolio adds $100 million to a firm's earnings. An investment banker who structures a transaction incorrectly can quickly transform a large acquisition from a brilliant idea to a $200 billion albatross.

Second, managers in financial firms generally believe they can identify the employees who drive good or bad results. Many important decisions and tasks are the responsibility of a single individual or small team, and the results of their actions are easy to observe. And, critically, managers typically believe a successful employee will continue to produce large profits.

Third, it is relatively easy for financial executives to move from one firm to another because they rarely rely on firm-specific inputs such as particular machines, patented processes, or other unique forms of capital. When there are synergies within a group of workers, such as an investment-banking team, the whole group can move from employer to employer. This mobility gives employees great bargaining power when negotiating their compensation.

In short, small differences in skill can produce enormous differences in profits, managers believe they can identify these differences in skill, and it is easy for a valued employee to be as productive at another firm. Because of these forces, particularly talented financial employees are able to retain a substantial portion of the large contribution they make to their employer's success. The result is millions in annual pay for top performers.

It is worth noting the parallels between the most highly paid financial managers and those at the top of many other professions, including actors, musicians, and athletes. A gifted actress, for example, can have an enormous impact on ticket sales when she stars in a movie, and her contribution to the movie's success is apparent on the screen. Moreover, experienced actresses can capture much of their value added: if one studio will not meet a star's price, she can easily move on to the next project. Indeed, compensation for top entertainers and athletes often exceeds compensation for top financial executives.

As a result of the Crisis, policymakers around the world are considering proposals to limit the compensation of financial executives. Economic logic and history both tell us, however, that market prices are typically the best way to allocate resources. If policymakers distort those signals, highly talented workers are less likely to find their most productive occupation. This would slow growth in economy-wide output and average standards of living.

Limits on the level of compensation in the financial services industry are also likely to trigger unintended and undesirable consequences. Pay caps imposed on a subset of firms, for example, could push their most talented bankers, traders, and other key professionals to unregulated firms. Broader limits on the compensation of financial executives may even drive parts of this highly mobile industry to more receptive countries.

Past efforts to cap executive compensation have often created unexpected problems, including, in some cases, an increase in the pay of those whose wages were meant to be constrained. A 1982 law aimed at limiting golden parachute payments in the United States paradoxically extended their use to new firms and new situations. In particular, firms discovered they could circumvent the new taxes on golden parachute payments by extending the payments to all terminations without cause, not just those associated with a change in control. Similarly, a 1993 American law aimed at limiting the tax deductibility of executive salaries sparked the proliferation of riskier option-based compensation.[2] Today the difficulty remains the same: regulating the level of compensation for financial executives could do more harm than good, both to the firms being regulated and to the overall economy.

The market does not allocate human capital perfectly, but it almost certainly does a better job than government officials would. This argument leads to our first recommendation.

RECOMMENDATION 1. *Governments should not regulate the level of executive compensation in financial firms.*

Bailouts during the World Financial Crisis have left governments as the dominant shareholder in many financial institutions. Standard governance arguments suggest that, while they are shareholders, governments representing the economic interest of taxpayers should advise management about compensation and related strategic issues. In principle, they should do so with the objective of maximizing the value of taxpayers' stakes in financial institutions. Broader political considerations should not distort management decisions. This could be achieved by having shareholder governments delegate compensation decisions to third parties, such as firms that advise boards and shareholders on executive compensation.

Our recommendation that governments should avoid regulating the level of compensation is not a rejection of proposals intended to improve corporate governance, such as say-on-pay votes and tighter standards of independence for compensation committee members. Such proposals may make corporations more productive by increasing management's incentives to act in the long-term interest of shareholders. However, as we emphasize below, changes that reduce the conflict between management and shareholders can magnify the conflict between financial institutions and society. This is an example of the more general point that regulations can easily have costly unintended consequences.

DEFERRED COMPENSATION: CHANGING THE STRUCTURE OF EXECUTIVE COMPENSATION TO REDUCE RISK TAKING AND THE POSSIBILITY OF TAXPAYER BAILOUTS

Although regulators should generally not set the level of compensation for financial executives, the possibility that governments will bail out financial firms during a crisis implies that stakeholders in financial firms—executives, creditors, and shareholders—do not face the full cost of their failure. As a result, these institutions have an incentive to take more risks than they would if they bore all the costs of failure. This in turn increases the likelihood of bank failures, the potential for systemic risk, and expected taxpayer costs.

A major goal of capital-market reform should be to force financial firms to bear the full cost of their actions. We propose several mechanisms to help achieve this goal. In the previous chapter, we recommend systemically sensitive capital requirements that force larger and more complex banks to hold more capital. In the next chapter, we advocate the creation of a long-term debt instrument that converts to equity during a crisis so that an undercapitalized or insolvent bank can transform into a well-capitalized bank at no cost to taxpayers.

Executive compensation presents an additional mechanism for inducing financial firms to internalize the costs of their actions. Specifically, if a significant portion of senior management's compensation is deferred and contingent on the firm surviving without extraordinary government assistance, managers will be less inclined to pursue risky strategies.

RECOMMENDATION 2. *Systemically important financial institutions should withhold a significant share of each senior manager's total annual compensation for several years. The withheld compensation should not take the form of stock or stock options. Rather, each holdback should be for a fixed dollar amount, and employees would forfeit their* *holdbacks if their firm goes bankrupt or receives extraordinary government assistance.*

In effect, holdbacks force employees to provide insurance against their firm's failure. Like any other insurance provider, they earn a fixed amount (akin to an insurance premium) if the firm does well, and bear a loss if the firm does poorly. As a result, this deferred compensation leans against management's incentive to pursue risky strategies that might result in government bailouts. Similarly, rather than wait for a bailout during a financial crisis, the management of a troubled firm would have a powerful incentive to find a private solution, perhaps by boosting the firm's liquidity to prevent a run, raising new capital, or facilitating a takeover by another firm. Because taxpayer losses trigger executive losses, holdbacks better align the personal incentives of managers with the fiscal and systemic goals of taxpayers.

More familiar forms of deferred compensation, such as stock awards and options, do little to reduce the conflict between systemically important financial institutions and society. Managers who receive stock become more aligned with stockholders, but this does not align them with taxpayers. Managers and stockholders both capture the upside when things go well, and transfer at least some of the losses to taxpayers when things go badly. Stock options give managers even more incentive to take risk. Thus, compensation that is deferred to satisfy this regulatory obligation should be for a fixed monetary amount. For example, firms might be required to withhold 20 percent of the estimated dollar value of each executive's annual compensation, including cash, stock, and option grants, for five years. At the end of this period, employees would receive the fixed dollar amount of their deferred compensation if the firm has not declared bankruptcy or received extraordinary government support.

Regulators need to specify clearly what events would trigger the loss of holdbacks. The triggers should include capital injections like those of the Troubled Asset Relief Program. Another should be unusual guarantees by the government of a firm's debt. Triggering events should not include less extreme events, such as borrowing from the Federal Reserve discount window.

Resignation from the firm should not accelerate the payment of an employee's holdbacks. Accelerating payment for employees who quit would weaken their concern about the long-term consequences of their actions. Moreover, it could create an incentive to quit, particularly if the employee discovers the firm may be in trouble. In the same spirit, managers should not be rewarded for taking their firm into bankruptcy. If a firm declares bankruptcy, its managers should receive their holdbacks only after its other creditors have been made whole.

This positioning of managers' claims means that a firm's obligation to pay deferred compensation does not affect its payments to other creditors in bankruptcy. Moreover, managers have no reason to push their firm into bankruptcy in an effort to collect compensation holdbacks. Thus, commitments to pay accumulated holdbacks do not put the financial institution or its other creditors at risk. Assets the firm holds to pay these obligations are capital that is available to pay other debts. Large firms that implement aggressive holdbacks can boost by billions of dollars the capital they have available to buffer against a major shock.

CONCLUSION

Executive compensation in financial firms is often faulted for the World Financial Crisis. We draw an important distinction between the *level* and the *structure* of executive compensation. Governments should generally not regulate the level of executive compensation in financial institutions. However, governments have a legitimate interest in the structure of executive compensation in financial firms. To force financial institutions to bear the full social cost of their actions, we recommend that government regulators require systemically important financial firms to hold back for several years a fraction of each employee's annual compensation. Employees would forfeit these holdbacks if the firm declares bankruptcy or receives extraordinary government assistance.

Compensation holdbacks are not a panacea. No single tool can perfectly align the incentives of stakeholders in financial companies with society's desire to avoid systemic financial distress. However, transparent compensation holdbacks with clearly specified trigger mechanisms would help avoid ad hoc measures such as those taken during the World Financial Crisis.

NOTES

1. Of course, governments are currently the dominant shareholder in many banks around the world, and while they are, it may be appropriate for them to advise management on compensation and other strategic issues. We discuss this issue below.
2. Kevin J. Murphy discusses these examples in his testimony, "Compensation Structure and Systemic Risk," before the U.S. House of Representatives Committee on Financial Services (June 11, 2009).

Chapter 7

An Expedited Mechanism to Recapitalize Distressed Financial Firms: Regulatory Hybrid Securities

---

This chapter develops a proposal aimed at sounder restructuring of distressed financial companies. We recommend support for a new regulatory hybrid security that will expedite the recapitalization of banks. This instrument resembles long-term debt in normal times but converts to equity when the financial system and the issuing bank are both under financial stress. The goal is to avoid ad hoc measures such as those taken during the World Financial Crisis, which are costly to taxpayers and may turn out to be limited in effectiveness. The regulatory hybrid security we envision would be transparent, less costly to taxpayers, and more effective.

WHY WE NEED EXPEDITED RESTRUCTURING MECHANISMS FOR DISTRESSED FINANCIAL FIRMS

Banks play an important and unique role in the economy. When banks are healthy, they channel savings into productive investments. When banks are unhealthy—whether undercapitalized or, even worse, insolvent—this role is compromised. Banks lend less, with adverse effects on investment, output, and employment. In response, governments often intervene to try to rehabilitate troubled banks during financial crises. As we discuss in Chapter 5, there are several reasons why these institutions may not recapitalize on their own.

First, after a bank has suffered substantial losses, managers who represent the interests of shareholders may be reluctant to issue new equity because of the debt overhang problem. Second, banks that are troubled but still satisfy regulatory capital requirements may decide it is in their interest to hold out for a government bailout. If a bank believes the government will not allow it to fail—and that the terms of a bailout will not be too onerous—management may choose to play chicken with the regulators, waiting for a government intervention rather than finding a private solution.

Finally, banking is a business founded on confidence; bankruptcy reorganization or an out-of-court workout is often not a viable option if a problem bank is to remain a going concern. The complexity of bank liabilities, the importance of short-term financing, and the transactional nature of many of their business relationships make it difficult for these institutions to survive a distressed restructuring. Even the threat of a restructuring may cause clients to flee and short-term creditors to withdraw their capital.

In this respect, banks and other leveraged financial firms are special. Most troubled nonfinancial firms can restructure—in or out of bankruptcy—by reducing or eliminating the claims of existing stockholders and converting debt into equity. As we saw with Lehman Brothers, however, distress for a financial firm usually leads to partial or complete liquidation (selling parts of the company to new owners) rather than a restructuring that would return the company to economic viability.

In short, because of the debt overhang problem and the possibility of a government bailout, banks prefer to reduce lending, sell assets if possible, or simply wait, rather than recapitalize themselves and maintain their lending capacity. And when financial firms do get into significant financial trouble, the standard restructuring process is typically ineffective and disruptive. If enough banks are affected and new banks or healthy banks cannot expand quickly enough, the resulting disruption of credit markets can lead to a significant economic slowdown.

Once a crisis hits, governments often try to prop up the financial sector through interventions such as those we witnessed during the World Financial Crisis. The U.S. Treasury, for example, made equity investments on terms that were typically attractive to banks, the FDIC guaranteed debt issued by banks, and the Federal Reserve purchased the "troubled" assets of several large financial institutions. Interventions such as these are problematic. They are made at great cost to taxpayers. They are also ad hoc and thus difficult for capital market participants to anticipate, which stifles recapitalization by those participants. The resulting uncertainty inhibits essential risk sharing, borrowing, and lending.

A more systematic and predictable approach would be better. For example, the FDIC's resolution mechanism avoids many of the costs associated with a standard bankruptcy. By quickly changing bondholders into stockholders and, when necessary, quickly transferring assets to healthy firms, the FDIC minimizes the economic disruption of a failed bank. Systemic financial risk is not restricted to banks. In the World Financial Crisis, for example, the government made massive transfers to AIG because of concerns about the effect a failure of this insurance company would have on the economy. Thus, it may be necessary to extend this expedited mechanism to a larger set of financial firms, as Federal Reserve Chairman Ben Bernanke has recommended.

Although FDIC regulators try to avoid disruptions when resolving a troubled bank, disruptions do inevitably occur and may impair the value of the bank's assets. It would be better if intervention were not necessary. Toward this end, we propose a complementary resolution mechanism: a new security that would allow a quick and minimally disruptive recapitalization of distressed banks.[1]

RECOMMENDATIONS

When large financial firms become distressed, it is difficult to restructure them as ongoing institutions. As a result, governments hoping to sustain their critical financial system are willing to spend enormous resources during economic crises to prop up failing financial institutions. We propose a new financial instrument, which we call a regulatory hybrid security, that will make it easier for troubled financial institutions to restructure. This security will also help society avoid paying for the mistakes of these institutions.

RECOMMENDATION 1. *The government should promote a long-term debt instrument that converts to equity under specific conditions.*[2] *Banks would issue these bonds before a crisis and, if triggered, the automatic conversion of debt into equity would transform an undercapitalized or insolvent bank into a well-capitalized bank at no cost to taxpayers. The costs would be borne by those who should bear them— the banks' investors.*

Conversion would automatically recapitalize banks quickly with minimal disruptions to operations. Freed of an excessive debt burden, banks would be able to raise more private capital to fund operations. They would not need capital infusions from the government, and the government would not have to acquire the assets of troubled banks. Finally, the prospect of a conversion of long-term debt to equity is likely to make short-term creditors and other counterparties more confident about a bank's future.

If this hybrid security is a good idea, why don't banks already issue it? The answer is that traditional debt is more attractive to banks because they do not have to bear the full systemic costs of leverage. This conflict between private and social costs is particularly severe for banks that consider themselves too big to fail. The prospect of a government bailout lets them ignore part of the cost of the risky actions they take—such as issuing debt—while cap-turing all the benefits. Because our regulatory hybrid security shifts the cost of risky activities back where it belongs, financial firms will be reluctant to issue such debt. To overcome this hurdle, government regulators must aggressively encourage the use of regulatory hybrid securities.

These regulatory hybrid securities will not prevent failure altogether, because banks also make other commitments, such as accepting deposits and issuing short-term debt. After the new hybrid instrument converts to equity, if the value of a bank's other commitments exceeds the value of its assets, additional complementary resolution mechanisms, such as an FDIC takeover, may be needed.

RECOMMENDATION 2. *A bank's hybrid securities should convert from debt to equity only if two conditions are met. The first requirement is a declaration by the systemic regulator that the financial system is suffering from a systemic crisis. The second is a violation by the bank of covenants in the hybrid security contract.*

The double trigger is important for two reasons. First, debt is valuable in a bank's capital structure because it provides an important disciplining force for management. The possibility that the hybrid security will conveniently morph from debt to equity whenever the bank suffers significant losses would undermine this productive discipline. If conversion is limited to only systemic crises, the hybrid security will provide the same benefit as debt in all but the most extreme periods.

Second, the bank-specific component of the trigger is also important. If conversion were triggered solely by the declaration of a systemic crisis, the systemic regulator would face enormous political pressure when deciding whether to make such a declaration. Replacing regulatory discretion with an objective criterion creates more problems because the aggregate data regulators might use for such a trigger are likely to be imprecise, subject to revisions, and measured with time lags. And, perhaps most important, if conversion depended on only a systemic trigger, even sound banks would be forced to convert in a crisis. This would dull the incentive for these banks to remain sound.

What sort of covenant would make sense for the bank-specific trigger? One possibility, which we find appealing, would be based on the measures used to determine a bank's capital adequacy, such as the ratio of Tier 1 capital to risk-adjusted assets.

In addition to the triggers, this new instrument will have to specify the rate at which the debt converts into equity. The conversion rate might depend, for example, on the market value of equity or on the market value of both equity and the hybrid security. Conversions based on market values, however, can create opportunities for manipulation. Bondholders might try to push the stock price down by shorting the stock, for example, so they would receive a larger slice of the equity in the conversion. Using the average stock price over a longer period, such as the past twenty days, to measure the value of equity makes this manipulation more difficult, but it opens the door for another manipulation. If the stock price falls precipitously during a systemic crisis, management might intentionally violate the trigger and force conversion at a stale price that now looks good to the stockholders. Finally, in some circumstances, a conversion ratio that depends on the stock price can lead to a "death spiral," in which the dilution of the existing stockholders' claims that would occur in a conversion lowers the stock price, which leads to more dilution, which lowers the price even further.

An alternative approach is to convert each dollar of debt into a fixed quantity of equity shares rather than a fixed value of equity. There are at least two advantages to such an approach. First, because the number of shares to be issued in a conversion is fixed, death spirals are not a problem. Second, although management might consider triggering conversion (for example, by acquiring a large number of risky assets) to avoid a required interest or principal payment on the debt, this would not be optimal unless the stock price were so low that the shares to be issued were worth less than the bond payment. Thus, management would want to intentionally induce conversion only when the bank is struggling. The advantages and disadvantages of different conversion schemes are complicated, however, and require both further study and detailed input from the financial and regulatory community.

CONCLUSION

To improve the restructuring of distressed financial companies, we recommend regulatory support for a new hybrid security that would expedite the recapitalization of banks. Banks would issue this debt before a crisis and, if a pre-specified covenant were violated during a systemic crisis, its automatic conversion into equity would transform an undercapitalized or insolvent bank into a well-capitalized bank at no cost to taxpayers.

Our regulatory hybrid security would help avoid ad hoc measures such as those taken during the World Financial Crisis. It would be transparent, with a clearly contracted trigger mechanism. It would be less costly to taxpayers because it would appropriately place recapitalization costs on banks' investors. And it would be more effective than recent measures, to the benefit of the overall financial system.

NOTES

1. Regulators impose capital requirements on financial institutions to reduce the likelihood these institutions will become distressed. In Chapter 5, we argue that regulators should consider systemic effects when designing capital requirements.
2. This mechanism is closely related to one proposed by Mark J. Flannery, "No Pain, No Gain? Effecting Market Discipline via 'Reverse Convertible Debentures,'" in Hal S. Scott, ed., *Capital Adequacy Beyond Basel: Banking, Securities, and Insurance* (Oxford: Oxford University Press, 2005).

Chapter 8

Improving Resolution Options for Systemically Important Financial Institutions

---

The World Financial Crisis revealed critical holes in the existing regulatory framework for handling large complex financial institutions that become impaired. First, regulators may not have the legal authority to do what is necessary to resolve a distressed institution's problems, including selling some divisions, closing or liquidating others, renegotiating or abrogating some contracts, and finding parties to manage what is left. Second, even if regulators have the necessary authority over part of the institution, they may not have authority over the whole firm. Holding companies, for example, often have subsidiaries that are incorporated in multiple countries and therefore are governed by different legal codes. Third, regulators are unlikely to be aware of all the interconnections within the institution and between the institution's various subsidiaries and other firms. This uncertainty makes it difficult for regulators to know the best way to restructure a financial institution, or indeed, whether restructuring is even feasible without enormous disruption.

We endorse legislation that would give authorities the necessary powers to effect an orderly resolution. As part of this authority, every large complex financial institution should be required to create its own rapid resolution plans, which would be subject to periodic regulatory scrutiny. These "living wills" would help authorities anticipate and address the difficulties that might arise in a resolution. Required levels of capital should depend in part on what the living wills imply about the time required to close an institution. This would create an incentive for financial institutions to make their organizational and contractual structures simpler and easier to dismantle.

RESTRUCTURING RATHER THAN BAILING OUT A DISTRESSED INSTITUTION: PRINCIPLES

Our recommendations are intended to allow regulators to deal with an impaired institution without necessarily having to provide additional assistance. Restructuring a distressed firm that is undercapitalized but solvent involves many complicated trade-offs and potential strategies. But once an institution is insolvent it is usually better to unwind it, salvaging the parts that have value and closing the rest, rather than propping up the firm with taxpayer funds.

Regulators typically face huge legal impediments, however, that prevent them from unwinding large complex and interconnected institutions. The connections between bank and non-bank subsidiaries of a single holding company, for example, make it difficult to identify all the bank's liabilities. The bank may depend on other subsidiaries of its holding company for critical services. If the holding company is declared bankrupt, the contracts governing the provision of these services may become invalid. The problems are magnified if the holding company has subsidiaries in different countries, with legal systems that differ in the way creditors are treated in the event of a failure and in the tools that can be used by authorities. As a result, the tried and tested resolution procedures that are used to wind down traditional deposit-taking banks cannot easily be adapted to resolve the problems of large and complex distressed financial institutions.

Many authorities support changes that would allow governments to shut down a bank holding company or other financial entity that has multiple subsidiaries operating in different lines of business and possibly in different countries. Harmonizing resolution procedures across international jurisdictions will be challenging, however, and the problem is made even more difficult if the burden of losses is to be shared by multiple governments. Paraphrasing Mervyn King, governor of the Bank of England, international banks are global in life but national in death.

As we have noted in previous chapters, the standard bankruptcy process does not work well for financial institutions because creditors and clients can flee at the first sign of trouble. Nonfinancial companies rarely lose their main customers and suppliers as soon as rumors of trouble surface. But as we saw during the World Financial Crisis, even hundred-year-old financial institutions are vulnerable to debilitating bank runs. As a result, the measured pace of normal bankruptcy procedures makes them inappropriate for financial institutions.

The government should instead have a resolution procedure that allows it to intervene quickly, to honor some contracts and to invoke contingencies in others. The resolution procedure should specify the types of contracts that must include clauses that can be invoked in a resolution event. The idea is to provide each institution and its counterparties with guidance about what can be expected during resolution, and to reduce the uncertainty that would otherwise exist if the regulators had total discretion. An improved resolution procedure would allow private parties to develop better contracts that anticipate the outcomes that might occur during resolution. For instance, the regulatory hybrid securities proposed in Chapter 7 would need to specify what the owners receive if the securities have not been converted to equity before a firm is unwound. This contingency must be addressed before the securities are issued.

The resolution procedure should be transparent, objective, and well understood by the private sector. It should allow regulators to liquidate an entity in an orderly fashion if that is necessary, or to rehabilitate part of an institution while winding down the rest. As with the bankruptcy rules that apply in most situations around the world, regulators would be required to make sure that no party whose contracts are adjusted would receive less than it would be entitled to if the institution were liquidated. Thus, the regulator's authority to adjust contracts would be like that of a bankruptcy judge, but would be invoked under specialized rules and with much less delay.

The absence of this authority costs taxpayers in several ways. First, it forces the government to bail out some institutions that would be closed or restructured if regulators had the authority to do so. Second, the fact that it is difficult for regulators to close large complex institutions creates incentives for banks to become large and complex. This in turn increases the frequency of bailouts and the cost when they do occur. Third, when negotiating with regulators about the size of a potential bailout, a distressed bank can hold out for more taxpayer support, because the government cannot credibly threaten to restructure the bank involuntarily. All of these problems raise the exposure of taxpayers and make the financial system less stable.

RECOMMENDATIONS

RECOMMENDATION 1. *We endorse efforts to create a better resolution procedure for systemically important institutions. Moreover, because of the importance of this issue, regulators should be granted the authority to restructure financial institutions as soon as possible.*

RECOMMENDATION 2. *Negotiations to create a unified cross-country resolution process should begin immediately. These negotiations should not, however, delay the implementation of interim regulations in each country that are as effective as possible, given existing cross-country differences.*

Qualifying "executory contracts," which include the majority of over-the-counter derivatives and standard repurchase agreements, are exempt in bankruptcy from automatic stays, and may therefore be settled before other claims against a bankrupt firm. This exemption contributes to the smooth functioning of the markets for these contracts, but it can also lead to substantial costs in bankruptcy. As we explain in the appendix to this chapter, replacing the exemption with a discretionary system in bankruptcy could seriously impair the normal functioning of the swap and repo markets. This leads to our third recommendation:

RECOMMENDATION 3. *The treatment of qualifying executory contracts in resolution should be specified precisely and should not be left to the discretion of regulators. The exemption currently given to these contracts should be reevaluated to determine if it unnecessarily adds to systemic risk.* We provide background on the issue of qualifying executory contracts in the appendix to this chapter.

PLANNING FOR THE DEMISE OF A MAJOR FINANCIAL INSTITUTION

Creation of a new cross-country process for restructuring complex and possibly multinational financial institutions will take time. There is one valuable tool, however, that can be deployed now. Every major bank holding company should be required to regularly file a "living will" detailing how the bank should be legally resolved in the event of distress. Other systemically important institutions monitored by the systemic regulator should also file these plans.

If the living will is invoked, the authorities will be trying to decide whether to close the institution or provide support. This could involve selling some parts of the institution, shuttering others, and preserving the rest. Uncertainty about (1) how the institution is connected to other institutions and (2) how the creditors and counterparties of the organization will react to these changes is one of the biggest factors that lead to bailouts. A living will would reduce this uncertainty.

The plan should include several components. The central element should be an assessment by management of the number of days necessary to resolve the firm without using regulatory intervention. This assessment represents an estimate of the time the firm would be in various bankruptcy courts around the world, including delays for potential pitfalls. The plan should describe the steps that would be required to restructure the firm and should highlight possible difficulties that could slow down the process. The description of how an unwinding could take place would help regulators in at least two ways. First, it would highlight solutions that do not require regulatory intervention. Currently these possibilities are based on considerable guesswork, which makes panics more likely. Second, if regulators do step in, the plan would show them where they should focus their attention.

The estimates of the days required to resolve the firm, especially the initial estimates, will be rough. But the risk managers of major financial institutions should already have some idea about the main bottlenecks they face. Also, the plans should be revised and updated regularly in conjunction with ongoing discussions between the institutions and the systemic regulator. The regulator must have the right to fine an institution if its plan is not properly prepared and documented. Thus, over time the estimates should become more meaningful and comparable across firms. The plan should also include the following elements:

- Detailed and full descriptions of the institution's ownership structure, assets, liabilities, contractual obligations, and the legal code that governs each major contract; descriptions of the cross-guarantees tied to different securities; a list of major counterparties; and a process for determining where the firm's collateral is pledged [1]
- A few major distress scenarios, and the likely resolution processes under each scenario
- A list of potential parties that could take over the institution's contractual obligations at low cost

The plans should be updated and reviewed by the systemic regulator at least once per quarter. Crucial parts of the plan (at a minimum, the number of days needed for resolution and the main impediments to or uncertainties associated with promptly dismantling the institution) should be summarized in public disclosures; this information would fit naturally in the risk management disclosures that are already standard items made available to the public. Most of the other information, however, should remain private, shared only with the regulators.

Over the medium term, the plans could be integrated with other parts of the regulatory architecture to deliver additional benefits. Longer periods for a standard resolution increase the cost of the resolution, both for the institution and for the economy, and increase the incentive for a government bailout. Thus, capital requirements should be higher for banks that require more time to restructure and close. This would give management a strong incentive to streamline its plans. We expect that the information about living wills in public disclosures would be valuable to equity analysts and external corporate governance advisers, allowing them to compare banks on the speed of their plans and on the main bottlenecks that would impede restructuring.

The first set of filings may uncover legal nightmares that would be impossible for regulators to anticipate. Many of the largest interventions during the World Financial Crisis occurred with little warning, under very tight deadlines. Living wills would have allowed regulators to anticipate the steps needed in these interventions. Other market participants might have more confidence in the entire financial system if they understood that a carefully designed plan would be the starting point for handling failing institutions.

We do not, of course, want to suggest that the actual resolution of a troubled institution will proceed exactly as envisioned in its living will. Many new issues and unanticipated problems are sure to crop up. The process of bargaining with the firm's creditors, counterparties, and potential acquirers cannot be scripted. But by offering a well-documented starting point, as well as some alternative paths devised in calmer times, the living will can simplify the process.

Many of our proposals are aimed at making bank failures less likely and less costly to the taxpayer. Living wills would complement these proposals. We suggest, for example, that capital requirements should depend on the size of an institution, the liquidity of its assets, and the degree to which it is funded with short-term debt. Higher capital requirements for organizations whose living wills suggest that their dismantling will be difficult are based on the same logic.

Similarly, the goal of the regulatory hybrid securities we advocate is to shift the cost of recapitalizing a struggling institution from taxpayers to the institution's owners. We expect the securities to convert to equity well before regulators intervene to close an institution and begin implementing the living will. After a conversion, the regulators would have time to scrutinize the will and explore its details in the context of the current crisis. During this time, the additional capital created by the conversion would allow the institution to comply with capital standards without having to sell assets. In short, easier resolution of an institution is a public good that benefits society but not necessarily bank owners. Thus, our fourth recommendation is as follows:

ADDITIONAL RECOMMENDATIONS

RECOMMENDATION 4. *All major bank holding companies and other large complex financial institutions designated by the systemic regulator should be required to file a living will ev-*

ery quarter. This set of detailed instructions should explain how the institution could be legally dismantled in the event of its failure.

Each country's systemic regulator should scrutinize the plans for the institutions in its jurisdiction to find emerging risks. Living wills would provide an early warning about new systemic risks and give regulators an opportunity to understand important new products. By comparing institutions, the regulators could also push laggards to match the steps taken by the leading institutions.

We are leery of additional mandates that could prove costly for financial institutions. We think living wills, however, score well on the ratio of value of information generated relative to the cost of producing it. There will no doubt be start-up costs in organizing the reports, but once in place, the marginal cost of continuing to update the plan should be low. In contrast, for all the reasons outlined above, the marginal benefits should remain large.

The Basel II framework already includes provisions regarding the monitoring of operational risk. A rapid resolution plan could, by regulatory decree, be required without the need for any legislation. Regulators of bank holding companies should immediately mandate that major bank holding companies prepare rapid resolution plans that contain all the elements described above. For systemic resolution in situations that are not constituted as bank holding companies, legislation should be passed to permit regulators of these entities to require rapid resolution plans.

Two further steps could enhance the operation of the new procedures. We offer them as additional recommendations.

RECOMMENDATION 5. *Banks whose plans suggest longer periods for a "standard" resolution should be required to hold more capital or to have a larger fraction of liabilities—such as regulatory convertible debt—that can be converted to equity without invoking bankruptcy.*

RECOMMENDATION 6. *The systemic regulator should be required to review the resolution plans each quarter and compare plans across institutions to ensure that all institutions have acceptable plans. The systemic regulator should have the authority to fine institutions whose plans are deficient.*

APPENDIX: THE SPECIAL CHALLENGES OF QUALIFYING EXECUTORY CONTRACTS

The demise of an institution that has substantial amounts of certain types of financial contracts can create many technical problems beyond those identified in the body of this chapter. These problems could cause spillovers that threaten the stability of the whole financial sector if a sufficiently large institution were to be declared bankrupt under existing laws. The proposed new forms of resolution authority do not, on their own, eliminate these problems.

Two important problems are associated with swap contracts and repurchase agreements. Many participants in the swap market have argued that they would not use swaps if the contracts were at risk for uncertain settlement as part of a bankruptcy proceeding. In deference to these arguments, the normal bankruptcy process does not apply to swaps. In particular, swap counterparties can net positions, access collateral quickly, and close out positions without being exposed to the possibly lengthy legal stays that apply to other creditors of a bankrupt firm. When positions are closed, the amount owed is determined by the master agreement between the parties. Typically, nondefaulting swap counterparties have the right to the replacement cost of their positions. The special treatment of these contracts can provide incentives to structure derivative contracts as swaps.

The transaction costs associated with settling swap contracts at bankruptcy can be enormous. For instance, suppose entities A and B have a swap contract that, based on the current mid-market price (between the bid and ask prices), implies entity A owes entity B $100. If B goes bankrupt, A does not settle its position with B by simply paying B $100 in cash. Instead, A is entitled to set up the same derivative position with another counterparty and pay B what it receives for the new position. Firm A will typically establish the new position at the bid price, which is below the mid-market price of $100, Thus, A will receive—and pay B—something less than $100—perhaps $99. In this scenario, 1 percent of the money owed to B would be lost.

Suppose B also has an offsetting swap with firm C. On this contract, B owes C $100 on a mid-market basis. When B goes bankrupt, C will probably have to pay a bit more than $100, say $101, to reestablish its position with another counterparty. Thus, C would present B with a bill for its net replacement cost of $101. In short, B's offsetting long and short contracts with A and C—which simply cancel each other if B survives—cost B the bid-ask spread when it goes bankrupt. More generally, B's total bankruptcy costs from its swap contracts is the total *gross* value of its positions multiplied by half their effective average bid-ask spread. Most large financial institutions have many offsetting positions that are fine-tuned to yield little net exposure to critical risks, but the gross value of the contracts is large. For example, the largest market participant, J.P. Morgan Chase, had about $80 trillion (according to the latest reports from the Office of the Comptroller of the Currency) in total outstanding derivatives contracts; the total market size is estimated at roughly $600 trillion. Thus, even ignoring the chaos associated with the rebalancing of huge portfolios, the failure of any of the large players in these markets would dissipate tens of billions of dollars merely in transaction costs. Moreover, as nondefaulting counterparties seek to replace their positions elsewhere in the market, they can destabilize price behavior, with potential knock-on effects. These problems can be mitigated with the use of central clearing.

A different problem arises with repurchase agreements when failure becomes a concern. Repurchase agreements are effectively collateralized loans, with most maturing on the next business day. Were default to occur, the lenders' claim on the pledged collateral is senior to the claims of all other creditors. Despite this priority, the potential cost of having the collateral trapped in a bankruptcy proceeding for even a short period is large relative to the interest due on a one-day loan. Moreover, despite the haircut taken when the collateral is established, there is some chance that the value of the collateral will drop below the value of the loan on the same day the borrower defaults. As a result, if a firm's short-term creditors believe there is a nontrivial chance it will fail, most will not roll over their loans when they mature. Those that remain will insist on collateral whose market value is quite certain. Short-term U.S. Treasury securities may continue to be accepted, but more volatile securities will no longer be accepted. As seen in the case of Bear Stearns, the result is essentially a run on the borrower.

NOTE

1. A cross-guarantee is a covenant that links multiple contracts. Typically, a cross-guarantee states that if a party defaults on one contract, the terms of a second contract change. For example, the second contract may become immediately payable.

Chapter 9

Credit Default Swaps, Clearinghouses, and Exchanges

As its name suggests, the payoff on a credit default swap (CDS) depends on the default of a specific borrower, such as a corporation, or of a specific security, such as a bond. The value of these instruments is especially sensitive to the state of the overall economy. If the economy moves toward a recession, for example, the likelihood of defaults increases and the expected payoff on credit default swaps can rise quickly. The Depository Trust and Clearing Corporation (DTCC) estimates that in March 2010, the notional amount of credit default swaps outstanding was about $25 trillion. As a result of the overall size of the CDS market and the sensitivity of CDS payoffs to economic conditions, large exposures to credit default swaps can create substantial systemic risk.

Because of this potential for systemic risk, some have argued that credit default swaps should be cleared through central clearing counterparties, or clearinghouses. In this chapter we analyze the market for credit default swaps and make specific recommendations about appropriate roles for clearinghouses and about how they should be organized. Clearinghouses are not a panacea, and the benefits they offer will be reduced if there are too many of them. Further, clearinghouses that manage only credit default swaps but not other kinds of derivative contracts may actually increase counterparty and systemic risk, contrary to the assumption of many policymakers.

THE MARKET FOR CREDIT DEFAULT SWAPS

A CDS can be viewed as an insurance contract that provides protection against a specific default. CDS contracts provide protection against the default of a corporation, sovereign nation, mortgage payers, and other borrowers. The buyer of protection makes periodic payments, analogous to insurance premiums, at the CDS rate specified in the contract. If the named borrower defaults, the seller of protection must pay the difference between the principal amount covered by the CDS and the market value of the debt. When Lehman Brothers defaulted, for example, its debt was worth about 8 cents on the dollar, so sellers of protection had to pay about 92 cents for each notional dollar of debt they had guaranteed.

Although credit default swaps can be used as insurance against a default, the buyer of protection is not required to own the named borrower's debt or to be otherwise exposed to the borrower's default. Both buyers and sellers may use credit default swaps to speculate on a firm's prospects. Some have suggested that investors should not be allowed to purchase CDS protection unless they are hedging exposure to the named borrower. We do not agree. Buying and selling credit default swaps without the underlying bond is like buying and selling equity or index options without the underlying security. Eliminating this form of speculation would make CDS markets less liquid, increasing the cost of trading and making CDS rate quotes a less reliable source of information about the prospects of named borrowers.

Credit default swaps are currently traded over the counter (OTC), rather than on an exchange. Each contract is negotiated privately between the two counterparties. CDS counterparties typically post collateral to guarantee that they will fulfill their obligations. (According to data from the International Swaps and Derivatives Association, about two-thirds of CDS positions are collateralized.) The collateral posted against a position is usually adjusted when the market value of the position changes. For example, if the estimated market value of a CDS contract to the buyer of protection rises—perhaps because the probability of default rises or the expected payment in the event of default rises—the seller of protection may be required to post additional collateral.

CLEARINGHOUSES, COUNTERPARTY RISK, AND SYSTEMIC RISK

Although credit default swaps can be valuable tools for managing risk, they can also contribute to systemic risk. One concern is that systemically important institutions may suffer devastating losses on large unhedged CDS positions. Counterparty risk, which arises when one party to a contract may not be able to fulfill its commitment to the other, is also a systemic concern. The failure of one important participant in the CDS market could destabilize the financial system by inflicting significant losses on many trading partners simultaneously. Derivatives dealers, for example, are on one side or the other of most CDS trades and, according to data from the DTCC, dealers hold large CDS positions. If a large dealer fails, whether because of CDS losses or not, counterparties with claims against the dealer that are not fully collateralized may also be exposed to substantial losses. The immense losses AIG suffered on credit default swaps during the World Financial Crisis (and the resulting increase in the collateral it was obligated to post) are a more vivid example of systemic risk. Apparently, regulators decided to bail out AIG after its losses because they feared that some of AIG's CDS counterparties would be irreparably harmed if AIG were unable to fulfill its commitments. Of course, financial institutions try to control their exposure to such losses, but risk management can fail.

After two counterparties agree on the terms of a CDS, they can "clear" the CDS by having a clearinghouse stand between them, acting as the buyer of protection for one counterparty and the seller of protection to the other. Once the swap is cleared, the original counterparties are insulated from direct exposure to each other's default and rely instead on the performance of the clearinghouse. Thus, with adequate capitalization, the clearinghouse can reduce systemic risk by insulating the financial system from the failure of large participants in the CDS market.

A clearinghouse not only insulates one counterparty from the default of another, it can lower the loss if a counterparty does default. Suppose, to pick an ideal example, that Dealer A has an exposure on credit derivatives to Dealer B of $1 billion, before considering collateral. That is, if Dealer B fails, then A would lose $1 billion. Likewise, B has an exposure to Dealer C of $1 billion, and C has an exposure to A of $1 billion. Without a clearinghouse, default by A, B, or C leads to a loss of $1 billion. With clearing, however, the positive and negative exposures of each counterparty cancel, and each poses no risk to anyone, including the clearinghouse. In practice, counterparty exposures are to some degree collateralized. This lowers the potential losses from a default, but collateral is expensive and only partially offsets counterparty risk.

This simple example illustrates two important advantages of clearinghouses. First, by allowing an institution with offsetting position values to net their exposures, clearinghouses reduce levels of risk and the demand for collateral, a precious resource, especially during a financial crisis. Second, by standing between counterparties and requiring each of them to post appropriate collateral, a well-capitalized clearinghouse prevents counterparty defaults from propagating into the financial system. Because of these advantages, pending U.S. legislation mandates that, with some exceptions, credit default swaps must be cleared.

Clearinghouses, however, are not panaceas. As for-profit institutions that compete for market share, they may be driven to lower their operating standards, demanding less collateral from their customers and requiring less capital from their members. *To ensure that clearinghouses reduce rather than magnify systemic risk, regulatory approval should require strong operational controls, appropriate collateral requirements, and sufficient capital. Clearinghouses should be subject to ongoing regulatory oversight that is appropriate for highly systemic institutions.*

Most of the systemic advantages of a clearinghouse require standardized contracts. The CDS losses AIG suffered in the World Financial Crisis again illustrate the point. Most of their credit default swaps were customized to specific packages of mortgages and would not have met any reasonable test of standardization. As a result, they would not have satisfied the requirements for clearing under any of the current clearinghouse proposals. AIG's failure was driven by its concentrated position in credit default swaps and by the fact that its huge bets were not recognized or acted upon by either its regulators or its counterparties. Only better risk management by AIG, better supervisory oversight by its regulators, or clearer disclosure of its positions to counterparties would have prevented the AIG catastrophe, even if clearinghouses for credit derivatives had been in place years ago. (We discuss AIG further in Chapter 11.)

One should not conclude that a ban on nonstandardized contracts is appropriate. An important function of financial institutions and insurance companies is precisely to meet the needs of individual businesses and owners of specific idiosyncratic securities for nonstandardized contracts. However, under the oversight of their regulators, those institutions must regularly evaluate and hedge the systematic risks of their retail businesses. Not doing so was the central failure that led to the AIG fiasco.

Because well-functioning clearinghouses can reduce systemic risk, financial institutions should be encouraged to use them to clear credit default swaps and other derivatives contracts. Banks and other regulated financial institutions should have higher capital requirements for contracts that are not cleared through a recognized clearinghouse. Financial institutions should not be required to clear all their CDS trades. Such a requirement would stifle innovation and possibly destroy the market for customized CDS contracts. Appropriate differences between capital requirements for contracts that are cleared and contracts that are not cleared will create the right incentives for firms to internalize the costs created by nonstandard contracts.

HOW MANY CLEARINGHOUSES?

Although competition created by multiple clearinghouses might lead to lower clearing fees and technical efficiencies, important opportunities to net offsetting credit default swaps may be lost if clearing is scattered across several institutions.[1] At the time we write this report, two CDS clearinghouses in the United States and five in Europe have already been established or proposed. It would be difficult if not impossible to net long and short positions that are cleared through different institutions. In the example above, Dealer B will be unable to net its contracts with A and C unless both contracts are cleared at the same clearinghouse. (With sufficient standardization of contracts, collateral, and risk management, netting across clearinghouses might be feasible, but this is not part of any of the existing proposals.)

Other netting opportunities will be lost if clearinghouses are dedicated solely to credit default swaps. In addition to their CDS positions, the major dealers also have large positions in interest rate swaps and other OTC derivatives. Most credit default swaps are part of a master swap agreement in which the two counterparties net their aggregate bilateral exposure across multiple contracts. If two dealers clear a CDS through a clearinghouse dedicated to credit default swaps, they cannot net their exposure from this contract against their exposures from other non-CDS contracts.

The potential benefits from netting credit default swaps against other types of contracts are large. According to the Bank for International Settlements, dealer exposures on interest rate swaps, for example, are about three times larger than those from credit default swaps. Research by Duffie and Zhu suggests that, given the size of these and other OTC derivatives markets in 2009, a dedicated CDS clearinghouse would actually *increase* average counterparty exposures. In essence, if the clearinghouse is limited to only credit default swaps, the increased opportunities to net CDS positions within the clearinghouse are dominated by the lost opportunities to net CDS positions against other derivatives contracts outside the clearinghouse. Duffie and Zhu also demonstrate that, even if the introduction of a dedicated clearinghouse reduces average counterparty exposures, adding a second clearinghouse dedicated to the same class of derivatives must increase average exposures. Finally, any increase in average counterparty exposure will be accompanied by more demand for collateral (a scarce resource) and for contributions to clearinghouse guarantee funds. (In the United States, the CME Group's proposal integrates clearing of credit default swaps with financial futures, somewhat mitigating this concern. However, interest rate swaps continue to trade OTC, and current proposals do not integrate them with CDS clearing.)

In short, widespread use of a dedicated CDS clearinghouse or fragmentation of clearing across several competing institutions will reduce the opportunities to net offsetting exposures. This will increase counterparty risk and, in turn, systemic risk.

A single clearinghouse for all OTC derivatives also has drawbacks. First, the competition created by multiple clearinghouses is likely to lead to innovation, more efficient operations, and lower cost. Second, even well-capitalized clearinghouses can fail. The failure of a clearinghouse for all OTC derivatives is likely to have enormous systemic consequences. *Despite these drawbacks, regulators and lawmakers should not intentionally or unintentionally promote the proliferation of redundant or specialized clearinghouses. The proliferation of clearinghouses would create unnecessary systemic risk by eliminating opportunities to reduce counterparty risk.*

EXCHANGE TRADING OF CREDIT DEFAULT SWAPS?

Although clearing does not require exchange trading, some have suggested that CDS trading should be conducted only on exchanges, which offer clearing and superior price transparency. Because the current OTC market is relatively opaque, in many cases bid-ask spreads are likely to shrink if trading moves to an exchange. This benefit, however, should be weighed against the benefits of innovation and customization that are typical of the OTC market.

Most important, requiring exchange trading for all credit default swaps is impractical. These contracts are traded on an enormous number of named borrowers and specific financial instruments. The DTCC provides data, for example, on the outstanding amounts of credit default swaps on 1,000 different corporate and sovereign borrowers. Although the most actively traded default swaps, such as CDS index products, are natural candidates for exchange trading, many less active swaps would not be viable on an exchange.

An attractive alternative to mandatory exchange trading is regulation that improves the transparency of trading for more active and standardized CDS contracts in the OTC market. U.S. dealers trading corporate and municipal bonds in the OTC market must quickly disclose the terms of most trades through TRACE, a reporting system maintained by the Financial Industry Regulatory Authority. Recent research suggests that dissemination of trade data through TRACE reduces the bid-ask spreads for some important classes of bonds.[2]

A similar system in the CDS market would increase the transparency of trades and improve the ability of participants to gauge the liquidity of the market and of regulators to identify potential trouble spots. Although increased transparency can in some cases limit market depth and stifle innovation, the benefits of greater transparency for established and active standardized contracts almost certainly exceed the costs. Industry efforts to achieve greater transparency in the CDS markets have been helpful and should be pursued aggressively. These efforts have improved competition by increasing awareness of trade prices and volume, but they have not been as successful in providing information about liquidity and trading costs. *Serious consideration should therefore be given to the introduction of a reporting system for the more active standardized index and single-name contracts, similar to the TRACE reporting system for corporate and municipal bonds.* If implemented judiciously, such a system would improve the quality of the market for these contracts.

RECOMMENDATIONS

This analysis leads to four recommendations:

RECOMMENDATION 1. *Because well-functioning clearinghouses can reduce systemic risk, financial institutions* *should be encouraged to use them to clear credit default swaps and other derivatives contracts. Banks and other regulated financial institutions should have higher capital requirements for contracts that are not cleared through a recognized clearinghouse.*

RECOMMENDATION 2. *To ensure that clearinghouses reduce rather than magnify systemic risk, they should be required to have strong operational controls, appropriate collateral requirements, and sufficient capital.*

RECOMMENDATION 3. *Because the proliferation of clearinghouses would create unnecessary systemic risk by eliminating opportunities to reduce counterparty risk, regulators and lawmakers should not intentionally or unintentionally promote the proliferation of redundant or specialized clearinghouses.*

RECOMMENDATION 4. *Regulators should promote greater transparency in the CDS market for the more liquid and standardized index and single-name contracts. Consideration should be given to the introduction of a trade reporting system for these contracts similar to the TRACE system for corporate and municipal bond trades in the United States.*

NOTES

1. D. Duffie and H. Zhu, "Does a Central Clearing Counterparty Reduce Counterparty Risk?" (working paper, Graduate School of Business, Stanford University, July 1, 2009).

2. See H. Bessembinder and W. Maxwell, "Markets: Transparency and the Corporate Bond Market," *Journal of Economic Perspectives* 22 (2008): 217–34; A. K. Edwards, L. E. Harris, and M. S. Piwowar, "Corporate Bond Market Transaction Costs and Transparency," *Journal of Finance* 62 (June 2007): 1421–51; M. Goldstein, E. Hotchkiss, and E. Sirri, "Transparency and Liquidity: A Controlled Experiment on Corporate Bonds," *Review of Financial Studies* 20 (2007): 235–73; and R. Green, B. Hollifield, and N. Schurhoff, "Financial Intermediation and the Costs of Trading in an Opaque Market," *Review of Financial Studies* 20 (2007): 275–314.

Chapter 10

Prime Brokers, Derivatives Dealers, and Runs

As we discuss in Chapter 1, runs by prime brokerage clients and derivatives counterparties were a central cause of the World Financial Crisis. Worried about potential losses, many clients withdrew their assets from brokerage accounts at Bear Stearns and Lehman Brothers in the weeks before these banks failed. Although Morgan Stanley did not fail, it also suffered from the withdrawal of prime brokerage assets. These runs, together with runs by short-term creditors, precipitated Bear Stearns' and Lehman's demise.[1] Even if these firms would have failed anyway, the runs made their failures much more sudden and chaotic, and made coherent policy responses much harder.

In this chapter we consider why clients ran, how such runs precipitated failure by substantially reducing the broker's liquidity, and what changes might ameliorate this unstable situation.

Two conditions are needed to generate a run. First, customers must have the incentive to withdraw their assets before bankruptcy occurs, and at least the quickest ones must have the ability to do so. Second, customer withdrawals must weaken the broker's financial position, making failure more likely and reinforcing the incentive for customers to claim their assets.

"Prime brokerage" is the package of services that securities broker-dealers offer to large active investors, especially hedge funds. These services typically include trade execution, settlement, accounting and other record keeping, financing, and, critically, holding the customers' cash and securities.

The relationship between a prime broker and its clients has the two features necessary for a run. First, even though securities entrusted to a prime broker belong to the client, it can be difficult or impossible for the client to extract its securities once the prime broker fails. As a result, customers are likely to withdraw their assets at the first sign that their prime broker is in difficulty. Second, as we explain below, prime brokers often use their clients' assets as an important access to funding or "liquidity." When a substantial number of clients leave, the broker must either find new financing quickly or sell assets to raise capital. As a result, concern that a prime broker is in trouble can be self-fulfilling.

Over-the-counter (OTC) derivatives relationships pose a similar problem. OTC counterparties have incentives to withdraw or restructure their contracts if they suspect the broker will fail. And the collateral provided by OTC derivatives counterparties is another important source of dealer liquidity.

Large broker-dealers are widely considered to be systemically important, so the potential for runs is a problem for the financial system. Regulatory changes that (1) reduce the incentive for customers to run, (2) reduce the liquidity effects of the decision to run, and (3) reduce the reliance of broker-dealers on run-prone financing can make the financial system more stable. These changes are worth making if the benefits to society exceed the costs to dealers, their customers, and the rest of the industry.

Our recommendations focus on segregation of assets. A customer's assets are segregated from those of its broker if the assets are held in a separate account that is legally distinct from the broker's accounts. If its assets are not segregated, the customer merely holds a contractual claim against the broker. In the event of bankruptcy by the broker, the customer owning nonsegregated assets may need to pursue claims against the dealer in court. Thus, segregation reduces the client's incentive to run.

The market for prime brokerage services is competitive and the customers are well informed. Thus, when prime brokers and their customers use nonsegregated accounts, we can infer that the private costs of segregation outweigh the private benefits. Because of the potential systemic cost of a run, however, the broker and its customers do not bear all the costs of their decision to use nonsegregated accounts.

To encourage greater segregation, we recommend higher regulatory liquidity requirements for dealer banks that use the assets of clients and counterparties as a source of liquidity. We also recommend the international harmonization of segregation regulations to prevent a "race to the bottom." This approach is more focused on the essence of the problem than are the simple constraints on size or activity that are sometimes advocated. We also warn against policy interventions that can increase the chance of runs.

PRIME BROKERAGE ASSETS

Broker-dealers depend on the assets of their prime brokerage customers for liquidity in two key ways. First, the dealer can offer cash loans to one client that are funded by cash held on deposit by another client.[2] Second, the dealer can pledge a customer's securities as collateral to obtain a loan from another bank or dealer. Such loans can finance the broker's own trading as well as loans to its customers.

Suppose Bank X has two prime brokerage clients, Hedge Funds A and B. It holds $250 million in cash belonging to Hedge Fund A. If Hedge Fund B requests a cash loan of $150 million, the broker can fund that loan from the $250 million deposited by Hedge Fund A. If Hedge Fund A moves its prime brokerage account to another bank, however, then Bank X must immediately find $150 million in new cash from other sources. (Bank X may be contractually entitled to demand that Hedge Fund B immediately repay its loan, but would be very unlikely to do so. Such an action would raise suspicions about Bank X's financial health and spark a worse run.)

Securities deposited with a prime brokerage are also a source of liquidity for the broker. Though these securities belong to the client and are not assets of the broker-dealer, the broker-dealer can use some of them as collateral for its own borrowing. If the client withdraws its assets, the broker must replace the collateral with uncommitted assets, which it may not have, sell assets on the market and repay the loan, or raise new capital by selling debt or equity. Because loans collateralized by securities typically come due at the start of the next business day, the broker needs to act quickly, even desperately. If, as is typically the case in a financial crisis, the markets for the broker's securities are illiquid, or the opportunity motivating its trades has gotten worse, the broker must close out its position at a loss, further weakening its financial position.

For example, in the quarters before the Lehman bankruptcy, Morgan Stanley reported that it held more than $800 billion in client assets that it could pledge as collateral. In its first disclosure after the bankruptcy, that figure had fallen to under $300 billion.[3] Not coincidentally, in the days following Lehman's failure, the "premium" for insuring Morgan Stanley debt in the CDS market rose sharply to above 10 percent per year.

There is nothing inherently nefarious or unethical about a prime broker using a client's assets to fund its own or other clients' activities. If a bank uses A's cash to fund a loan to B, it is in essence mediating lending from A to B. This raises the interest A receives on its cash, lowers the interest B pays for its loan, and generates fee income for the bank. If the bank uses A's securities as collateral, it can fund an original margin loan to A that lets A buy securities in the first place. It is in essence acting as intermediary for A's collateralized borrowing. And if A's securities are better collateral than the bank's, then using A's securities as collateral for the bank's own operations is simply a more efficient use of capital. The problem with using a client's assets in this way is that it makes the bank susceptible to a run, and the social costs of the run are likely to be greater than the costs to the individual parties.

Regulations in the United Kingdom allow prime brokers to commingle their clients' assets with their own. This leads to both a strong incentive to run and a strong effect on broker liquidity if there is a run. If the broker fails, the client can find itself unable to quickly retrieve assets that the broker has used as collateral for its own loans, since those assets now also "belong" to someone else.[4] Many former U.S.-based Lehman clients are still trying to regain the assets they had placed in Lehman accounts in London before the firm's bankruptcy.

Segregation rules in the United States are stricter. U.S. rules limit the amount of customer assets that can be "re-hypothecated," or used again as collateral for the broker's purposes, to 140 percent of the amount the dealer has lent the customer in cash. Thus, if a dealer lends a client $100 to buy $200 of securities, it can use $140 of those securities as collateral for its own loan.[5] Thus, despite the tighter U.S. rules, client assets are an important source of funding for prime brokers in the United States.

As in the United Kingdom, clients of a troubled prime broker in the United States have an incentive to run. Failure by a broker-dealer can subject levered investors, such as hedge funds, to substantial costs and delays. Even if a client eventually recovers all of its assets, the investor may remain exposed to market risks and unable to use the collateral value of its securities for weeks or months. Thus, clients of prime brokers in the United States and the United Kingdom are likely to flee with their assets at the first sign of trouble.

International competition is important in this market and must be considered in any regulatory response. Because regulations controlling the use of customer assets in the United States are tighter than those in the United Kingdom, U.S. banks often provide prime brokerage services through their London-based broker-dealer affiliates, and offer clients better terms for agreeing to this move. They can also offer better terms than custodian banks, where assets are fully segregated.

OTC DERIVATIVES COLLATERAL

Collateral provided under OTC derivatives contracts, such as interest rate swaps and credit default swaps, presents a similar set of issues.[6]

A counterparty to a derivatives dealer often provides an "independent amount" of collateral at the inception of a trade, which the dealer holds for the life of the position. Then, as the market value of the position moves, each counterparty provides additional collateral, dollar for dollar with the change in value of the contract. Typically, dealers do not demand an independent amount of collateral from corporate (nonfinancial) end users or from other dealers. The aggregate amount of collateral held by dealers from other clients is often substantial. For instance, the International Swaps and Derivatives Association reports that in 2008, approximately two-thirds of derivatives positions were collateralized.[7] Dealers are not required to segregate the collateral OTC derivatives counterparties post with them. They can use the collateral as an unrestricted source of financing. A dealer may use cash collateral, for example, to buy securities. As a result, if a dealer goes bankrupt, it may be difficult for its customers to quickly recover the independent-amount collateral. The customer will also worry that a bankrupt dealer may not perform on the primary payments of the derivative, such as CDS or interest rate swap payments.

Thus, once a dealer's viability is threatened, its OTC derivatives counterparties have an incentive to run by reducing their derivatives positions with the dealer. When they do, they can reclaim the independent amount of collateral that they had deposited with the dealer. They can also enter into contracts that require the dealer to pay cash to the customer, thus draining cash from the dealer. Dealers in financial difficulty will be reluctant to refuse such requests, since a refusal could signal liquidity problems and make the run worse. In turn, again, such withdrawals hurt the dealer's cash position, driving it further into trouble.

U.S. bankruptcy law grants most OTC derivatives an exemption from automatic stays during bankruptcy. Without this provision there would be even more runs than there are now. The less a derivatives counterparty worries about a broker's bankruptcy, the less incentive that counterparty has to run. However, the privileged position of OTC counterparties is not universally popular. After a bank has failed or been bailed out by the government, it is not obvious to other creditors why derivatives counterparties deserve to walk away with the first available dollars. Should new regulations expose derivatives counterparties to an automatic stay or other less favorable treatment, the risk of a flight of OTC derivatives counterparties from a weak dealer will rise.

Regulators are also likely to demand an increase in collateralization, to increase the "safety" of the system. Absent new regulations regarding the segregation of such collateral, dealers are also likely to use that collateral as a source of financing, and will find themselves in even more trouble when counterparties start to pull away from derivatives contracts.

RECOMMENDATIONS

The painful lessons taught by the World Financial Crisis have already reduced the amount of unsegregated hedge fund assets provided to prime brokers. Now wary, many hedge funds have been moving some of their assets into custodial accounts, in which securities are completely segregated and are not available to prime brokers as a source of financing, and some are spreading assets across multiple prime brokers.[8]

Nevertheless, it would be a mistake to assume that such learning, combined with the interests of the private parties involved, will be sufficient to eliminate forever prime brokerage runs as a threat to systemic stability. There is a clear externality. When a bank and a hedge fund agree to a prime brokerage arrangement with less segregation, both parties share in the financing benefits. There are additional risks to the two parties as well, of course, and these risks are now more evident.

However, because of the threat of runs created when assets are not segregated, taxpayers and society bear some of the costs of this arrangement. If the government intervenes because it fears "systemic" effects from the failure of the prime broker bank, taxpayer dollars are at risk. The failure of a truly systemic institution by definition carries costs for society as a whole. Finally, financial crises usually involve losses in output and employment, which lead to social costs beyond the raw costs of bailouts and other interventions. A prime broker and its clients do not consider these costs when deciding how carefully to segregate assets. (On the other hand, the free flow of rehypothecated securities may offer external benefits as well, by providing additional liquidity to markets.)

To make prime brokerage and OTC derivatives less run-prone, either or both of the central ingredients of a run must be addressed. There must be less incentive for customers to run, and withdrawals must cause less damage to the broker's financial strength.

Increased segregation of client assets is a natural recommendation that serves both purposes.

At a minimum, we recommend the following two changes:

RECOMMENDATION 1. *Regulators should impose and monitor liquidity requirements on systemically important banks and broker-dealers. To the extent that a bank or broker-dealer* *depends for short-term financing on its customer's assets (that is, if it does not segregate those assets), this financing source should be assumed to disappear when determining whether the bank and broker-dealer meets those liquidity requirements.*

RECOMMENDATION 2. *The prime brokerage regulations of the United Kingdom and other major financial centers should be tightened so that segregation requirements for customer assets are at least as restrictive as current U.S. requirements.*

The first recommendation gives an incentive to segregate but stops short of simply mandating segregation. An example of a liquidity requirement for banks, broker-dealers, and other regulated financial institutions is the minimum liquidity coverage ratio outlined by the Basel Committee in 2009.[9] The current Basel proposal does not, however, recognize that customer assets held by a prime broker are a source of liquidity that could disappear.

By increasing the liquidity requirements of firms that do not segregate, those firms feel some of the social costs, and also will have more sources of cash with which to withstand runs. The second recommendation ensures there will not be a regulatory "race to the bottom" in this international and interconnected market.

Alternative and stronger approaches may also be considered. One alternative is to require that assets be fully segregated, as they are when held in custodial accounts. Full segregation is cleaner, simpler, and easier to monitor. On the other hand, it imposes additional costs because it forces assets to sit idle when they could provide other services. Existing research does not provide good guidance that quantifies the benefits or the costs, so we do not take a position on full segregation.

We also warn against regulatory changes that make prime brokerage clients, derivatives counterparties, and short-term creditors more vulnerable in bankruptcy, and thus more prone to run.

NOTES

1. Darrell Duffie, "The Failure Mechanics of Large Dealer Banks," *Journal of Economic Perspectives* 24 (February 2010): 51–72.
2. SEC Rule 15c3-3 requires prime brokers in the United States to collect their clients' free credit balances "in safe areas of the broker-dealer's business related to servicing its customers" or to otherwise deposit the funds in a reserve bank account to prevent commingling of customer and firm funds. "Free credit balances" are the cash that a client has a right to demand on short notice. The text of the SEC rules is available on-line from multiple sources, including the *Securities Lawyer's Deskbook,* published by the University of Cincinnati College of Law. The text of Rule 15c3-2, on customers' free credit balances, can be found at http://www.law .uc.edu/CCL/34ActRls/rule15c3-2.html. Rule 15c3-3, on "Customer Protection—Reserves and Custody of Securities," can be found at http://www .law.uc.edu/CCL/34ActRls/rule15c3-3.html.
3. See Manmoham Singh and James Aitken, "Deleveraging after Lehman— Evidence from Reduced Rehypothecation" (unpublished working paper WP/09, International Monetary Fund, 2009); and Andrew Ross Sorkin, *Too Big to Fail* (New York: Viking, 2009).
4. Sean Farrell, "Hedge Funds with Billions Tied Up at Lehman Face Months of Uncertainty," *The Independent,* October 6, 2008; James Mackintosh, "Lehman Collapse Puts Prime Broker Model in Question," *Financial Times,* September 24, 2008; and Singh and Aitken, "Deleveraging after Lehman."
5. See Duffie, "The Failure Mechanics," for details.

6. In an interest rate swap, a customer may promise to pay a floating rate in exchange for a fixed rate of payments. If interest rates rise, payments flow from customer to bank, and the customer must post collateral to guarantee those payments. A credit default swap is essentially insurance on a bond: The buyer of protection pays a premium, say 2 percent of face value per year, and in return the seller of protection promises to cover a bond default. If the bond becomes riskier, the seller has to post additional collateral with the buyer, so that if the seller defaults the buyer can get a new contract at the now higher premium.

7. International Swaps and Derivatives Association, *ISDA Margin Survey 2009* (ISDA Technical Document, New York, 2009).

8. Brad Hintz, Luke Montgomery, and Vincent Curotto, *U.S. Securities Industry: Prime Brokerage, A Rapidly Evolving Industry* (technical report, Bernstein Research, March 13, 2009).

9. Basel Committee, "International Framework for Liquidity Risk Measurement, Standards and Monitoring" (Bank of International Settlements, Basel, December 17, 2009), http://www.bis.org/publ/bcbs165.pdf.

Chapter 11

Conclusions

THE TWO CENTRAL PRINCIPLES UNDERPINNING OUR INDIVIDUAL RECOMMENDATIONS

This book should be seen as our collective best answer to the question of how the financial system can be organized to facilitate economic growth without the need for recurring taxpayer support. Our answers are summarized in two broad principles.

The first principle is that, when developing and enforcing regulations, government officials must consider the implications not only for individual institutions but also for the financial system as a whole. Financial regulations in almost all countries have been designed to ensure that individual institutions, principally commercial banks, will remain sound when they suffer unexpected losses on their assets. This focus on individual firms ignores critical interactions between institutions. Attempts by individual institutions to remain solvent in a crisis, for example by selling assets, cutting back on loans to viable borrowers, or requiring more collateral, can undermine the stability of the system as a whole. The focus on individual firms can also cause regulators to overlook important changes in the overall financial system. For example, although the markets for securitized assets and the broader shadow banking system of lightly regulated financial institutions grew dramatically in the years before the current crisis, existing regulatory structures did not evolve with them.

Chapters 2 and 3 elaborate on this first principle. Chapter 2 argues that in each country, one regulatory organization—which, we argue, on balance, should be the central bank—should be responsible for overseeing the health and stability of the overall financial system. Chapter 3 argues that this systemic regulator needs a new infrastructure to collect and analyze adequate information from large and systemically important financial institutions. This new information framework would bolster the government's ability to foresee, contain, and ideally prevent disruptions to the overall financial services industry.

Chapter 4 suggests that the public may also benefit from the systematic provision of information. We recommend simple and standardized disclosures of risks in financial products, specifically in mutual funds used in tax-favored retirement accounts. Some commentators argue that weak public understanding of complex financial products contributed to the rapid growth in household debt that preceded the World Financial Crisis. While this claim is unproven, public trust in and understanding of the financial system are important for the functioning of an advanced economy. We believe that improved risk disclosures can contribute to such trust and understanding.

The early chapters of our book emphasize that regulators must take a broad view of the financial system, and must gather information that will allow them to do that. The experience of the World Financial Crisis suggests that strict regulation of a narrow portion of the financial system, such as the commercial banking industry, encourages migration of financial activities outside the regulated system to a shadow financial system whose risks are then poorly understood and inadequately monitored. Problems in the shadow system can cause financial instability both through connections with regulated institutions and because people come to rely on the shadow system to perform key financial functions such as risk transfer. Moreover, the successful separation of regulated from unregulated activities requires that the government commit itself in advance not to bail out the unregulated financial system in the event of a crisis, and that this commitment be credible. We doubt that such a credible commitment can be made.

Our second central principle is that regulators must create conditions that minimize the likelihood of bailouts of financial firms by forcing them to internalize the costs of failure they have been imposing on taxpayers and the broader economy. During the World Financial Crisis, several governments bailed out ailing financial firms through fiscal transfers and other mechanisms because they feared that these firms were too large or too systemic to fail without catastrophic costs. Many of our recommendations are intended to create a robust financial system in which any troubled financial company is allowed to fail.

Regulators should use many tools to make firms internalize systemic dangers and reduce the chance of a crisis, but capital requirements are among the most powerful. Financial institutions that create more systemic risk should have higher capital requirements. Capital reduces risk directly, by providing a buffer against losses, and indirectly, by forcing stockholders to bear the losses from risky strategies. Chapter 5 proposes systemically sensitive capital requirements that require larger and more complex banks to hold more capital.

Rather than relying only on shareholders to discipline the risk-taking tendencies of financial institutions, regulators should also impose costs of failure on the management of these institutions that are greater than those shareholders are likely to impose on their own. Chapter 6 argues that each systemically important financial institution should be required to withhold a significant share of each senior manager's total annual compensation for several years, with these holdbacks forfeited if the firm goes bankrupt or receives extraordinary government assistance.

Acknowledging that some financial firms will encounter problems, Chapters 7 and 8 propose better mechanisms for stabilizing or liquidating struggling firms. Chapter 7 argues for a new hybrid debt instrument that would expedite the recapitalization of banks at no cost to taxpayers: banks would issue this debt before a crisis and, if a pre-specified trigger were breached during a systemic crisis, the debt would automatically convert into equity. In this way, bondholders would bear the costs of failure when they should, rather than benefit from government bailouts or threaten the system with bankruptcies.

Although such recapitalizations would help firms avoid failure, they would not save every distressed firm. Accordingly, Chapter 8 argues that that each systemically important financial institution should be required to create and maintain for regulators a "living will" (subject to regular review) that highlights key complexities of its organizational and financing structure and lays out a plan for how it could be legally dismantled if it fails.

The World Financial Crisis, and specifically the failure of Lehman Brothers, revealed some important technical weaknesses in the financial system, specifically in the market for credit default swaps and the standard arrangements for prime brokerage, that contributed to the chaotic environment of late 2008. In Chapters 9 and 10 we suggest reforms of CDS clearing mechanisms and the structure of prime brokerage to address these technical vulnerabilities.

The measures we propose in Chapters 7 through 10 have two important effects. First, they make it much easier for governments to allow financial institutions to fail if a crisis does occur. Thus they directly reduce the likelihood of costly, ad hoc interventions. Second, to the extent that bondholders, shareholders, and managers of financial institutions understand that they are less likely to be bailed out in a crisis and, in the case of bondholders and managers, will suffer costs if such a bailout does occur, they will be more cautious beforehand. This will reduce the likelihood that a crisis occurs in the first place.

Taken together, our proposals would reduce both the likelihood and the severity of future financial crises. Existing rules in the United States and many other countries have led to ad hoc, emergency interventions to save unprofitable banks at great current and future cost to taxpayers and great collateral damage to the broader economy. We offer a robust regulatory system that would be less prone to crisis and would better allow struggling banks to fail.

REPLAYING THE WORLD FINANCIAL CRISIS: HOW OUR RECOMMENDATIONS MIGHT HAVE HELPED

How would the World Financial Crisis have played out had all our policy proposals been in place? Our answers are obviously speculative and benefit from 20/20 hindsight. They should not be interpreted as criticism of the actions of regulators and policymakers during a difficult and chaotic period. Nevertheless, the Crisis allows us to illustrate how our recommendations could work in practice.

The Buildup to the Crisis

We recommend that central banks assume the role of systemic regulator, empowered to "understand trends and emerging risks in the financial industry" and then "design and implement financial regulations with a systemic focus" (Chapter 2). We do not recommend that the systemic regulator should try to identify asset price bubbles. In fact, financial economists argue about whether reliable identification of bubbles is even possible in real time. However, dangerous buildups of leverage in the financial system, which sometimes accompany rising asset prices, are clearly an appropriate object of concern for regulators. Thus, it is likely that a systemic regulator would have devoted attention to the risks of historically unprecedented increases in residential real estate prices that were central to the World Financial Crisis.

Many central bankers were in fact keenly watching real estate and related derivatives in the years before the Crisis erupted. They did little, but as systemic regulators they would have had a responsibility to act. For example, a systemic focus on increasing leverage during the boom might have led to tangible actions that would have limited the origination of high-risk mortgages. More broadly, mandated annual "risk of the financial system" reports highlighting the risk to the financial system from unexpected decreases in housing prices (Chapter 3) might have induced more prudent choices among other regulators, financial firms, and home builders and buyers. This is a specific example of the potential benefit of risk reporting to improve public understanding of financial risks (Chapter 4).

Monitoring, reporting, and regulating systemic risk is challenging. Thus, the systemic regulator, which we argue should be the central bank, should be allocated resources for staff explicitly charged with analyzing the whole financial system. Even with this focus and these resources, we do not presume that systemic regulators can avoid all crises and related recessions—including the one just past. However, we do think that systemic regulators might have reduced some of the problems that created the World Financial Crisis.

One of the central goals of our recommendations is to eliminate expensive bailouts for financial firms. How would our policy recommendations have altered the nature and extent of support for five firms at the epicenter of the World Financial Crisis, Bear Stearns, Fannie Mae, Freddie Mac, AIG, and Lehman Brothers?

Bear Stearns

The Securities and Exchange Commission, Bear Stearns' main regulator, was not up to the task of supervising the firm. Indeed, the SEC Chairman infamously announced that all was fine with the company just 48 hours before it failed. Inadequate supervision meant that no one in government understood clearly Bear Stearns' balance sheet, funding strategy, or interconnections to the overall financial system.[1] Because of these problems, Bear Stearns' rescue was orchestrated using very incomplete information and very rough guesses about how failure might impair the financial system.

Our recommendations could have helped in three respects. First, from the perspective of the safety of the financial system, Bear Stearns was seriously undercapitalized. Public accounts of its demise emphasize the disagreement within the firm over whether to raise new equity or reduce risk.[2] Our proposals on capital rules (Chapter 5) would have forced Bear Stearns (and all other securities dealers) to have had more capital in the months and years leading up to the crisis. Our regulatory hybrid securities (Chapter 7) could also have been issued by Bear Stearns and converted in time to reduce its interest payments and debt overhang problems during this difficult time.

Second, our proposal for compensation holdbacks (Chapter 6) would have provided an additional buffer against taxpayer losses when Bear Stearns failed. It might also have changed the discussions within the firm about whether to cut risk exposure and raise capital during the early stages of the World Financial Crisis. In the five years before it was absorbed by J.P. Morgan, Bear Stearns paid over $17 billion in employee compensation and benefits. Our proposal for compensation holdbacks might have set aside $2 billion or more of this total.[3] In the Bear Stearns rescue, the Federal Reserve provided J.P. Morgan protection against losses on roughly $30 billion of Bear Stearns' hard-to-value securities. This guarantee was structured so that the Fed had a senior loan against the assets of $28.8 billion and J.P. Morgan had a junior loan of $1.15 billion. As of December 31, 2009, the fair-market value of these securities had fallen to $27.2 billion. Thus, compensation holdbacks would have materially reduced the Fed's risk on this loan.

At the time of Bear Stearns' takeover, its employees were estimated to have held more than 30 percent of its outstanding shares. Thus, Bear Stearns seems to have satisfied the often heard corporate-governance proposal for improving the incentives of executives by making employees hold their firm's shares. As we explain in Chapter 6, however, the key compensation issue from the perspective of systemic risk is *not* better aligning the incentives of managers with shareholders' incentives. Managers who receive stock become more aligned with stockholders, but this does not align them with society.

Third and finally, the systemic regulator would have been more familiar with Bear Stearns and its potential problems. For example, we recommend that the systemic regulator be the authority that monitors and approves living wills, in which financial institutions would identify potential low-cost buyers for key parts of their firms (Chapter 8). This living will information would have been valuable in arranging the distressed sale of Bear Stearns.

Fannie Mae and Freddie Mac

Unlike Bear Stearns, the problems of Fannie Mae and Freddie Mac were well understood by many government officials. For instance, starting in 2004, Federal Reserve Chairman Greenspan testified on several occasions about the risks posed by these firms.[4] After major accounting scandals at both firms, the Bush administration proposed legislation to revise their supervision. It could not get congressional support, however, and reform efforts stalled. Indeed, in late 2007 some members of Congress were calling for Fannie Mae and Freddie Mac to expand their operations to support the faltering housing market. Given the depth of support the two companies had over many years from many parts of the federal government, the existing regulatory system failed spectacularly to control their operations and overall systemic risk.

Fannie Mae and Freddie Mac have two lines of business. One is guaranteeing securitizations of prime mortgages that meet their underwriting standards. The other is holding a portfolio of mortgages and of mortgage backed securities that they themselves guarantee. This portfolio grew dramatically through the 1990s until leveling off in the early 2000s. Around that time, Fannie and Freddie began to build a large portfolio of lower-quality (subprime and alt-A) mortgages and the AAA tranches of securities backed by lower-quality mortgages. These purchases were seen by the enterprises as part of their mission to promote housing finance. However, because Fannie and Freddie operated with so little capital, once the housing market began to deteriorate, they had an inadequate buffer to protect against the losses in their portfolio and on the mortgage-backed securities they guaranteed. As of early 2010, the Congressional Budget Office estimates that taxpayer losses from these two institutions will exceed $300 billion.

It is clear that a competent systemic risk regulator would have flagged these institutions as a source of risk (Chapter 2). This regulator would then have had the authority to raise their capital requirements (Chapter 5). On closer examination, it also might have insisted on tighter rules for minimum down payments. These policies would likely have greatly reduced the ultimate taxpayer cost of these two firms.

Lehman Brothers

The Lehman Brothers bankruptcy remains one of the most controversial events of the World Financial Crisis. As the fourth largest investment bank, with more than $600 billion in assets at the time of its failure, our capital-requirement recommendations would have mandated that Lehman hold more capital during its pre-Crisis expansion because of both its size and its reliance on short-term funding (Chapter 5). The compensation holdbacks we propose would have generated more pressure for Lehman to find a buyer without government support (Chapter 6). And, like Bear Stearns,

Lehman could have issued regulatory hybrid securities that would have reduced its leverage amid its emerging distress in 2008 (Chapter 7).

The reporting requirements for our new information infrastructure would have required all major institutions to report their asset positions every quarter (Chapter 3). Armed with this information, as Lehman's condition worsened, regulators would have better understood the losses Lehman's counterparties would suffer if the firm failed and could have identified and alerted institutions with concentrated exposure to Lehman—and, as we discuss below, to AIG, which was rescued the day after Lehman failed.

Lehman's bankruptcy caused private sector losses that our regulatory proposals could have mitigated in at least three ways. First, the bankruptcy filing triggered an abrupt unwinding of all Lehman's derivative positions. Lehman was party to 1.2 million derivative contracts worth a total notional value of $39 trillion.[5] Our proposals would push derivative transactions toward centralized clearing. If Lehman's contracts had been cleared, the task of unwinding the positions would have been less urgent and less challenging.

Second, the bankruptcy filing created chaos in Lehman's brokerage and clearing operations because many of its customers' assets and securities had been commingled with Lehman's own assets. Customers have been left as general creditors in the ensuing bankruptcy, and many have yet to recover their money. Our recommendation that regulators tighten liquidity requirements for prime brokers (Chapter 10) might have induced greater segregation of customer assets within Lehman.

Third, the bankruptcy filing has been difficult because of the complexity of Lehman's global structure. Lehman was operating in more than 40 countries, with many activities run through London. When the firm's U.S. parent filed for bankruptcy, the British operation was immediately sent into administration. Lehman had more than 900 operating companies worldwide, and 16 different administrators are currently presiding over the bankruptcy in different jurisdictions. It will take years to resolve this case. Our proposals that firms like Lehman create and maintain living wills, and that countries strive to harmonize bankruptcy rules for systemically important financial institutions, could have streamlined Lehman's bankruptcy administration. We do not mean to overstate this, however. Negotiating a common set of rules will take many years, and resolving a large global firm like Lehman will take much time and effort under any regime.

Most important, had our proposals been in place and understood, expectations of a government bailout of Lehman would have been much lower, and the firm's failure would not have triggered a major change in expectations about the rest of the financial system.

American International Group

AIG's regulators were ill-equipped to understand the workings of AIG Financial Products, the subsidiary that wrote the derivatives that played a critical role in AIG's problems. AIG's financing crisis arose because many of its derivative contracts forced it to post large amounts of additional collateral if its credit ratings from Moody's and Standard and

Poor's were downgraded. When AIG's ratings were downgraded in September 2008 in the wake of Lehman's failure, AIG was required to post more than $13 billion in collateral. Although failure to post the collateral would have meant AIG was in default on its contracts, it was not able to raise funds quickly enough to do so. AIG had written more than $375 billion in credit default swaps, including $70 billion on CDOs, and was a significant counterparty to many of the financial system's most important firms. Its default would have led to significant losses for many of them. To prevent AIG's default, authorities rescued the firm the day after Lehman's bankruptcy.

A systemic regulator armed with the information and tools we propose could in many ways have helped AIG, taxpayers, and the overall financial system. Because of AIG's size, it would have faced substantially higher capital requirements as it grew in the years preceding the crisis (Chapter 5). Our proposed information infrastructure would have revealed its burgeoning unhedged CDS positions—information that, in turn, could have triggered the systemic regulator to initiate risk-control conversations with AIG management long before the fateful Lehman bankruptcy (Chapter 3). The regulators overseeing AIG Financial Products had no reason to consider how a failure of AIG would affect its counterparties, but a systemic regulator would have been responsible for assessing the firm's interactions with other systemically important institutions. AIG's living will would have discussed obvious distress scenarios—one of which likely would have been a rating-agency downgrade (Chapter 8). Compensation holdbacks might have raised the incentive of key AIG managers to limit the firm's growing risk (Chapter 6). Finally, by giving AIG an incentive to use and clear standardized CDS contracts, our recommendations would have reduced AIG's systemic importance (Chapter 9). A March 2010 estimate by the Congressional Budget Office puts the taxpayer cost of rescuing AIG at $36 billion. Our proposals would have substantially reduced this amount.

The net impact our recommendations would have made in the World Financial Crisis will always be uncertain and debatable. However, it seems reasonable to conclude that with these measures in place, many of the central features of the Crisis would have played out differently, with less damage to the overall financial system, lower cost to taxpayers, and perhaps better outcomes for key firms as well.

LIKELY CHALLENGES WITH IMPLEMENTING OUR RECOMMENDATIONS

Our full set of recommendations will require significant changes in laws and practices. Though our expertise is in financial economics rather than politics, we can anticipate several challenges that may impede these changes.

The economic hardships triggered by the World Financial Crisis have caused government officials and citizens around the world to demand regulatory reforms that will prevent financial crises. There is no reasonable way to accomplish this goal. Financial crises have recurred throughout modern history. The run-up and collapse of house prices in the recent

Crisis echo the speculation in tulip bulbs in the 1630s, in British railway stocks in the 1840s, and in Florida land in the 1920s. We expect that financial crises will continue to happen for centuries into the future. Our goal is not to prevent such crises but to reduce their frequency and severity. This goal is intellectually sound and attainable, but we acknowledge that it may seem underwhelming. Unreasonable expectations by the public, however, may keep legislators and regulators from enacting important changes that will reduce the conflict between financial firms and society.

Elected officials around the globe have been heavily criticized for many decisions made during the Crisis. Populist pressure in many countries has impeded discussion of even technical issues such as resolution reform. Some mistakenly claim, for example, that the intent of sensible bankruptcy reform is to enable future bailouts. Political rhetoric that reinforces this confusion delays meaningful change.

Most important, reform is often impeded by powerful interests with a stake in the status quo. We expect many financial institutions to resist our proposals. One of our central principles is that a financial firm's losses should be borne by its stakeholders, not by broader society. Recommendations that reduce the expected subsidy from taxpayers also reduce the expected wealth of stakeholders. Compensation holdbacks, for example, reduce management's incentive to take risks that might eventually be subsidized by taxpayer bailouts. Regulatory hybrid securities reduce the value of a financial institution by roughly the drop in the firm's expected subsidy from taxpayers. And higher capital requirements to protect the financial system lower the industry's bottom line. Our purpose is not to harm financial firms or their stakeholders. Indeed, robust financial institutions are critical for economic growth and rising standards of living. However, proposals to eliminate the socialization of losses that can occur in financial crises, and thereby make crises less likely, also would promote economic well-being.

Government regulators may also resist some of our proposals. We argue, for example, that central banks should be responsible for systemic regulation. In some countries this may require a transfer of existing authority from other agencies. In other countries it may conflict with the ambitions of other agencies seeking this role. Those agencies will fight against their loss of power and resources. Similarly, our recommendation for a new information infrastructure might force some regulators to share information they currently hoard.

Finally, our proposals would have their greatest benefit when they alter the behavior of financial institutions before a crisis occurs. This cannot happen unless the relevant decision-makers—financial executives, current and potential creditors, boards of directors—believe that the environment has truly changed. This will take time. It may also require the failure of one or more important financial firms without government bailouts for people to genuinely believe that a new regime is in place and that every large financial institution will not be bailed out.

These challenges can be met and overcome. With appropriate new regulations, financial firms can again resume their critical role of matching lenders with borrowers to help raise standards of living around the world. If new regulations are misguided, however, we will continue to be threatened by severe financial crises and the recessions and unemployment that often accompany them, or we will face the even worse prospect of an overregulated and politicized financial system that cannot support a dynamic growing economy. We all should hope that policymakers are up to the task. Our book aims to support this effort.

NOTES

1. See, for example, SEC Office of Inspector General, *SEC's Oversight of Bear Stearns and Related Entities: The Consolidated Supervised Entity Program*, SEC Report 446-A, September 25, 2008. This report would have received greater public attention had it not been released at the height of the World Financial Crisis.
2. Kate Kelly, "Lost Opportunities Haunt Final Days of Bear Stearns: Executives Bickered Over Raising Cash, Cutting Mortgages," *Wall Street Journal*, May 27, 2008, A1.
3. Compensation data taken from page 130 of the November 2007 Bear Stearns SEC 10K filing, http://www.bearstearns.com/includes/pdfs/investor_relations/proxy/10k2007.pdf.
4. Alan Greenspan, "Proposals for Improving the Regulation of the Housing Government Sponsored Enterprises," February 24, 2004, testimony to the Committee on Banking, Housing and Urban Affairs, U.S. Senate, 108th Cong., 1st sess., www.federalreserve.gov/boarddocs/testimony/2004/20040224/default.htm.
5. "The Specter of Lehman Shadows Trade Partners: Derivatives Pacts Remain in Limbo for Municipalities, Firms," *Wall Street Journal*, September 17, 2009, C1, http://online.wsj.com/article/SB125313981633417557.html.

Contributors

Martin N. Baily holds the Bernard L. Schwartz Chair in Economic Policy at The Brookings Institution. He was Chairman of the Council of Economic Advisers and a member of the cabinet in the Clinton Administration. He is a Senior Advisor to McKinsey and Company and the co-chair of the taskforce on financial reform convened by the Pew Charitable Trusts.

John Y. Campbell is the Morton L. and Carole S. Olshan Professor of Economics and Chair of the Department of Economics at Harvard University, and a former President of the American Finance Association. He is the author of *Strategic Asset Allocation: Portfolio Choice for Long-Term Investors* and *The Econometrics of Financial Markets* (Princeton).

John H. Cochrane is the AQR Capital Management Professor of Finance at the University of Chicago Booth School of Business, President of the American Finance Association, and a Research Associate of the National Bureau of Economic Research. He is the author of *Asset Pricing* (Princeton).

Douglas W. Diamond is the Merton H. Miller Distinguished Service Professor of Finance at the University of Chicago's Booth School of Business. He is a Fellow of the American

Academy of Arts and Sciences and the Econometric Society, and has served as President of the American Finance Association.

Darrell Duffie is the Dean Witter Distinguished Professor of Finance at Stanford University's Graduate School of Business. He was the President of the American Finance Association in 2009, and is the author of *Dynamic Asset Pricing Theory* (Princeton).

Kenneth R. French is the Carl E. and Catherine M. Heidt Professor of Finance at the Tuck School of Business, Dartmouth College. He is a Fellow of the American Academy of Arts and Sciences, and was President of the American Finance Association in 2007.

Anil K Kashyap is the Edward Eagle Brown Professor of Economics and Finance at University of Chicago Booth School of Business. He is also currently a consultant or advisor to Federal Reserve Banks of Chicago and New York, the U.S. Congressional Budget Office, and the Cabinet Office of the Japanese Government.

Frederic S. Mishkin is the Alfred Lerner Professor of Banking and Financial Institutions at the Graduate School of Business, Columbia University. He was a member (governor) of the Board of Governors of the Federal Reserve System from 2006 to 2008, and is the author of *The Next Great Globalization: How Disadvantaged Nations Can Harness Their Financial Systems to Get Rich* (Princeton).

Raghuram G. Rajan is the Eric J. Gleacher Distinguished Service Professor of Finance at the University of Chicago's Booth School of Business. He is currently President (Elect) of the American Finance Association, an economic advisor to the Prime Minister of India, and served as the chief economist of the International Monetary Fund from 2003 to 2006. He is the author of *Fault Lines: How Hidden Fractures Still Threaten the World Economy* and (with Luigi Zingales) *Saving Capitalism from the Capitalists* (both Princeton).

David S. Scharfstein is the Edmund Cogswell Converse Professor of Finance and Banking at Harvard Business School. His research has focused on banking, financial distress, corporate investment, and risk management.

Robert J. Shiller is the Arthur M. Okun Professor of Economics, Cowles Foundation and School of Management, Yale University, and author of seven books, including *Irrational Exuberance* (Princeton). He is the co-creator, with Karl E. Case, of the Standard & Poor's/Case-Shiller Home Price Indices.

Hyun Song Shin is the Hughes-Rogers Professor of Economics at Princeton University. In 2010, he is on leave serving as an economic adviser to the South Korean President.

Matthew J. Slaughter is the Associate Dean of the MBA Program and the Signal Companies Professor of Management at the Tuck School of Business at Dartmouth. From 2005 to 2007, he served as a member on the Council of Economic Advisers.

Jeremy C. Stein is the Moise Y. Safra Professor of Economics at Harvard University. He was President of the American Finance Association in 2008. From February through July of 2009, he worked on financial stabilization and reform in the Obama Administration, serving as senior advisor to the Treasury Secretary, and on the staff of the National Economic Council.

René M. Stulz is Everett D. Reese Chair of Banking and Monetary Economics at the Fisher College of Business at the Ohio State University. He is a former editor of the *Journal of Finance* and a former president of the American Finance Association and a trustee of the Global Association of Risk Professionals.

Index

agency problems: capital requirements and, 72–74; conflicts of interest and, 16–21; financial system issues and, 16–21

American Finance Association, vii

American Home Mortgage Investment Corp., 3

American International Group (AIG), 89, 112; credit default swaps (CDS) and, 5, 25, 48, 114–15, 148–49; new information infrastructure and, 47–48; scenario of under recommended policy, 146–49

arbitrage, 10–11, 30nn4,7

Asia crisis of 1997–98, 27

asset backed securities, 7, 12–14, 47, 72

asset classification, 65n2

assets: liquidity and, 3, 10–12, 19–22, 28, 31n14, 35 (see also liquidity); prime brokerage, 125–28; recapitalization and, 86–94; reforming capital requirements and, 67–74; segregated, 124–33, 146

auction rate securities, 3–4

bailouts, 7–8; capital requirements and, 69; competitive advantage from, 19–20; executive compensation and, 79–82; minimizing likelihood of, 137–40; policy recommendations for, 131, 137–42, 147, 150–51; recapitalization and, 87–91; resolution options and, 98–103; restructuring and, 96–99; scenario of under recommended policy, 141–42; too-big-to-fail policy and, 18–19, 21, 29, 90

Bank for International Settlements, viii, 116

Bank of England, viii, 97

bankruptcy: AIG, 5; American Home Mortgage Investment Corp., 3; bailouts and, 96 (see also bailouts); Barings Bank, 17; Bear Stearns, 4–5, 24–25, 33, 39, 108, 122, 142–45; Chapter 7 and, 22; Chapter 11 and, 22; conditions generating, 122–25; creditors and, 22; disorderly liquidation and, 22; executive compensation and, 82–84; Fannie Mae, 4–5, 14, 28, 142, 144–45; Freddie Mac, 4–5, 14, 28, 142, 144–45; holdbacks and, 82; Lehman Brothers, 4–6, 16, 25, 33, 47, 88, 110, 122, 126–27, 139, 142, 145–48; living wills and, 96, 100, 103–5, 139, 144, 147–48; Northern Rock, 3, 33, 39; over-the-counter (OTC) derivatives and, 129–30; politics and, 150; prime brokers and, 122–29, 133; recapitalization and, 87–89; resolution options and, 21–23, 95–108; restructuring and, 87–88; scenario of under recommended policy, 140–49; U.S. code on, 22

banks: asset liquidity and, 72–73; auction rate securities and, 3–4;

banks (*cont.*)
  bailout of, 7–9 (*see also* bailouts); central, 3, 19, 26–27, 34, 38–43, 136, 140–41, 151; confidence in, 87; conflicts of interest and, 16–21; contracted activity and, 12–16; covered interest parity and, 11; credit crunch and, 7–9, 12–16, 30n1; debt overhang and, 18, 88; delevering and, 10, 70; deposit insurance and, 23, 36, 41, 52, 70, 88–89; economic role of, 86–87; executive compensation and, 75–85; executory contract qualification and, 100, 106–8; Great Depression and, 23; hybrid securities and, 90–94; leverage and, 10, 14, 28, 87–90, 140–41, 146; living wills and, 96, 100–105, 139, 144, 147–48; planning for demise of major, 100–104; policy recommendation principles and, 135–40; prime brokerage assets and, 125–28; recapitalization of, 86–94; reforming capital requirements and, 67–74; resolution procedures and, 21–23; runs on, 23–25 (*see also* runs); shadow banking system and, 9–12, 33, 37, 42, 136–37; standardized position values and, 35; systemic regulator for, 33–43; too big to fail, 18–19, 21, 29, 90; underestimated risk and, 28
Banque de France, viii
Barings Bank, 17
Basel Committee, 132
Bear Stearns: failure of, 4–5, 24–25, 122; resolution options and, 108; scenario of under recommended policy, 142–45; systemic regulator for, 33, 40
Belgium, 8
Bernanke, Ben, 5, 31nn14,17, 89

BNP Paribas, 3
bonds: disruptions of normal pricing relations and, 11–12; hybrid securities and, 90–94. *See also* financial markets
bonuses, 21
Bush, George W., vii, 5, 144

call option, 12
capital: bank incentives to raise, 70
capital requirements: agency problems and, 72–74; asset liquidity and, 72–73; bailouts and, 69; bank size and, 71–72; competitiveness effects and, 69; disciplining effect of short-term debt and, 69; external financing and, 68; policy recommendations for, 71–74; shareholders and, 70; short-term debt and, 68–69, 72–74
central banks, 3, 19, 26–27; consumer protection and, 42; independence and, 39, 41; as lender of last resort, 39; long-run inflation targets and, 41; macroeconomic policy and, 39; mandates for, 40–43; policy recommendations for, 136, 140–41, 151; stability and, 39–41; as systemic regulator, 34, 39–43; trading relationships of, 39
Chari, V. V., 15
Christiano, Lawrence, 15
clearinghouses: collateral and, 114; counterparty risk and, 110–13, 116–17, 120; Depository Trust and Clearing Corporation (DTCC) and, 109, 112, 118; as for-profit institutions, 113–14; insulation by, 113; limitation of, 116–17; number of, 115–17; operating standards and, 113–15; other netting opportunities and, 116; over-the-counter (OTC) deriva-

tives and, 111, 117; policy recommendations for, 119–20; reform of, 110–20, 139; systemic risk and, 109–15; TRACE system and, 118–20

Clinton, Bill, vii

collateral, 5, 10, 24, 30n7; credit default swaps (CDS) and, 111–17, 120; interest rate swaps and, 134n6; over-the-counter (OTC) derivatives and, 123, 128–30; policy recommendations and, 135, 139, 147–48; prime brokerage assets and, 125–28; reform and, 68; resolution options and, 102, 106–7; systemic regulation and, 35, 41, 45–47

conflicts of interest, 16–21

Congressional Budget Office, 145, 149

Council of Economic Advisers, vii

counterparty risk, 45; AIG and, 112; clearinghouses and, 110–13, 116–17, 120; credit default swaps (CDS) and, 110–13, 116–17, 120; derivatives dealers and, 128–30; over-the-counter (OTC) derivatives and, 111, 117; resolution options and, 106–8

covered interest parity, 11

credit crunch, 7–9, 12–16, 30n1

credit default swaps (CDS): AIG and, 5, 25, 48, 114–15, 148–49; arbitrage and, 30n7; clearinghouses and, 110–20; collateralization rates and, 111; counterparty risk and, 110–13, 116–17, 120; Depository Trust and Clearing Corporation (DTCC) and, 109, 112, 118; description of, 109; destabilization by, 112; disruption of normal pricing relations and, 11–12; exchange trading of, 118–19; as insurance, 5, 110–11; interest rate

swaps and, 116–17, 128–29, 134n6; International Swaps and Derivatives Association and, 111, 128–29; Lehman Brothers and, 110; market for, 110–11; over-the-counter (OTC) derivatives and, 111, 117–18, 128–30; policy recommendations for, 119–20; prime brokerage assets and, 126; reform of, 110–20, 139; systemic risk and, 109–20; TRACE system and, 118–20; unhedged positions and, 111–12

Darwinian processes, 21

debt: Federal Deposit Insurance Corporation (FDIC) and, 88–89; hybrid securities and, 90–94; recapitalization and, 86–94; restructuring and, 96–108

debt overhang, 18, 70, 87–88, 142

default: counterparty risk and, 45; cross-guarantee and, 108n1; during World Financial Crisis, 1, 5, 8, 14, 29, 148; reforming capital requirements and, 67–68, 71–72. See also credit default swaps (CDS)

deferred compensation, 80–84

defined benefit pension plans, 53, 58

defined contribution plans, 53–55, 58, 61–63

deflation, 27

Democrats, viii

deposit insurance, 23, 36, 41, 52, 70, 88–89

Depository Trust and Clearing Corporation (DTCC), 109, 112, 118

derivative positions, 47–50

derivatives dealers, 25; collateral and, 128–30; credit default swaps (CDS) and, 110–20; new information infrastructure for, 47–50; over-the-counter (OTC) derivatives

derivatives dealers (*cont.*)
and, 123, 128–31; policy recommendations for, 130–33;
policy scenarios and, 141, 146–
47; resolution options for, 100,
106–8
drawdowns, 15–16
Duffie, D., 116–17

equity, 12; credit default swaps
(CDS) and, 111, executive compensation and, 81; hybrid securities and, 90–94; policy recommendations and, 138, 142; prime
brokers and, 126; recapitalization
and, 86–94, reforming capital
requirements and, 70; retirement
savings and, 63; resolution options and, 103–5; systemic regulation and, 36
European Central Bank, viii, 3, 18–19
European Commission, viii
European Union, 115–16
exchanges, 11, 111, 118–19
executive compensation: accountability and, 81–84; bailouts and,
79–82; bankruptcy and, 82; deferred compensation and, 80–84;
golden parachutes and, 79; holdbacks and, 81–84; level of, 75–77,
84; limitation of, 78–79; mobility
and, 77; policy recommendations for, 79–84; politics and, 80;
profits and, 77–78; reasons governments should not control, 76–
80, 85n1; regulation of, 75–85;
results-oriented, 77; shareholders and, 79–81, 85n1; skill and,
77–78; stock awards and, 81–83;
structure of, 75–76, 80–84; tax
deductibility and, 79; Troubled
Asset Relief Program (TARP)
and, 83
executory contract qualification,
100, 106–8

Fannie Mae, 4–5, 14, 28, 142, 144–45
Federal Deposit Insurance Corporation (FDIC), 36, 41, 52, 88–89
Federal Housing Finance Agency, 4
Federal Reserve, vii–viii; bank bailouts and, 7–9; Bear Stearns and,
4–5; Bernanke and, 5, 31nn14,17,
89; Greenspan and, 144; information infrastructure and, 48,
52; mortgage pooling and, 14;
systemic regulation and, 40;
Troubled Asset Relief Program
(TARP) and, 5, 7
Financial Industry Regulatory Authority, 118–19
financial institutions: bailouts and,
96–99 (*see also* bailouts); bankruptcy resolution procedures
and, 21–23; clearinghouses and,
110–20; conflicts of interest and,
16–21; credit default swaps (CDS)
and, 109–21; critical interactions
between, 33; debt overhang and,
18; deposit insurance and, 23,
36, 41, 52, 70, 88–89; executive
compensation and, 75–85; executory contract qualification and,
100, 106–8; expedited restructuring mechanisms for, 86–94;
holding companies and, 95–97,
100, 104–5; hybrid securities and,
90–94; individual firms and, 33–
34, 37, 45, 135–36; information
infrastructure for, 44–52; leverage
and, 10, 14, 28, 87–90, 140–41,
146; liquidity and, 3, 10–12, 19–
22, 28 (*see also* liquidity); living
wills and, 96, 100–101, 103–5,
139, 144, 147–48; planning for
demise of major, 100–104; policy
recommendation principles and,
135–40; recapitalization of distressed, 86–94; reforming capital
requirements and, 67–74; resolution options for, 95–108; share-

holders and, 16–21; too big to fail, 18–19, 21, 29, 90; TRACE system and, 118–20. *See also* banks
financial literacy, 57
financial markets: arbitrage and, 10–11, 30nn4,7; auction rate securities and, 3–4; bank bailouts and, 7–9 (*see also* bailouts); covered interest parity and, 11; credit crunch and, 7–9, 30n1; credit default swaps and, 109 (*see also* credit default swaps [CDS]); disruptions of normal pricing relations and, 11–12; economic welfare from, 1; flight to quality and, 8–9; hybrid securities and, 90–94; information infrastructure for, 44–52; retirement savings and, 53–66; Securities and Exchange Commission and, viii, 5, 36–37, 40, 48, 52, 55, 133n2, 142; shadow banking system and, 9–12, 33, 37, 42, 136–37; systemic regulator for, 33–43
Financial Services Authority (FSA), 40
financial system: agency issues and, 17–21; bailouts and, 7–8, 79–82, 87–90, 99–103, 131, 137–42, 147, 150–51; bankruptcy and, 21–23 (*see also* bankruptcy); conflicts of interest and, 17–21; improving resolution options for, 95–108; policy recommendation principles and, 135–40; prime brokers and, 24–25 (*see also* prime brokers); resolution procedures and, 21–23; serious problems with, 16–26; shocks and, 42, 84; systemic regulator for, 33–43; systemic risk and, 2, 19, 35–40, 43, 45, 47, 50, 69, 74n1, 76, 81, 101, 105, 109–20, 137, 141–45; technical weaknesses in, 139; World Financial Crisis and, 16–26 (*see also* World Financial Crisis)

fire-sale risk, 22, 31n14, 45–47, 52, 67–71
flight to quality, 8–9
Florida, 150
Fortis, 8
401(k) plans, 53, 58, 65n1, 66n4
Freddie Mac, 4–5, 14, 28, 142, 144–45
Futures Trading Commission, 52

Germany, 8
golden parachutes, 79
Goldman Sachs, 5
government: control of executive compensation and, 76–80; hybrid securities and, 90–94; resolution options and, 95–108. *See also* regulation
Great Depression, 1, 8, 16, 23–24
Greenspan, Alan, 144

hedge funds: clearinghouses and, 110–11, 115; long-short strategies and, 5; new information infrastructure and, 47, 49; policy recommendations for, 130–33, 148; prime brokers and, 24, 123–30; World Financial Crisis and, 10–11, 24, 30n7
Her Majesty's Treasury, viii
high-fee funds, 56, 59
holdbacks, 81–84, 138, 142–45, 148–50
holding companies, 95–97, 100, 104–5
housing, 4, 26–29, 141, 144–45, 145, 149
hybrid securities, 74n1; bailouts and, 90–91; conversion ratio and, 90–94; double trigger of, 91–92; goal of, 104; policy recommendations for, 89–93, 138, 142, 146, 150; politics and, 92; recapitalization and, 90–94; systemic regulator and, 35–36; Tier 1 capital and, 92
Hypo Real Estate Holdings, 8

Iceland, 8
inflation, 1, 41, 60, 65n2
information infrastructure: annual
   reports and, 51–52; counterparty
   risk and, 45, 106–8, 110–13, 116–
   17, 120; current information gaps
   and, 45–48; derivative positions
   and, 47–48; fire-sale risk and, 22,
   31n14, 45–47, 51, 67–71; general
   asset positions and, 47–49; individual institutions and, 45; lag
   and, 51; market enhancement
   from, 44; model-based valuations and, 50; new authority and,
   48–51; nutrition label model and,
   54, 58–65; policy recommendation principles and, 136; prime
   brokers and, 124; recommendations for, 48–52; retirement savings and, 53–66; sharing and,
   51; standardization and, 49–50,
   53–55, 58–65; TRACE system
   and, 118–20
ING, 8
interest rate swaps, 116–17, 128–29,
   134n6
Internal Revenue Service (IRS), 62
International Monetary Fund (IMF),
   vii
International Swaps and Derivatives
   Association, 111, 128–29
Ivashina, Victoria, 15

Japan, 12
Japanese-style deflation, 27
J.P. Morgan, 4, 143

Kehoe, Patrick, 15
Kerviel, Jérôme, 17
King, Mervyn, 97
Korea, viii
Kunreuther, Howard, 43n1

Leeson, Nick, 17
legal impediments to restructuring,
   96–97

Lehman Brothers, 33, 110, 126–27;
   complex global structure of, 147;
   drawdowns and, 15; information
   infrastructure and, 47; money
   market funds and, 25; policy
   recommendations and, 139, 142,
   145–48; recapitalization and, 88;
   regulatory inadequacy and, 25;
   run on, 4–6, 122
leverage, 10, 14, 28, 87–90, 140–41,
   146
liquidity, 88, 111; clearinghouses
   and, 119–20; information infrastructure and, 46; policy recommendations for, 124–25, 138, 146;
   prime brokers and, 122–32, 134n9;
   reforming capital requirements
   and, 72–74, 82; resolution options and, 95, 98, 104; runs and,
   122–32; short-term debt and, 68–
   69, 72–74; systemic regulation
   and, 35; World Financial Crisis
   and, 3, 10–12, 28, 31n14
living wills, 96, 100–101, 103–5, 139,
   144, 147–48
loans, 36, 52, 70, 88; collateral and,
   5, 10, 24, 30n7, 35, 41, 45–47, 68,
   102, 106–8, 111–17, 120, 123–30,
   134n6, 135, 139, 147–48; contracted activity and, 12–16; credit
   crunch and, 7–9, 12–16, 30n1;
   default and, 1, 5, 8, 14, 29, 67–68,
   71–72, 108n1; drawdown and,
   15–16; interbank, 3, 6; recapitalization and, 86–94
long-short strategies, 5
Luxembourg, 8

Medicaid, 56
Moody's, 147
moral hazard, 56
Morgan Stanley, 122, 126
mortgage backed securities, 3–5, 7,
   9, 70, 144–45
mortgages, 13–14, 28–29, 47, 114, 141
mutual funds, 6, 54, 65n3, 136

Netherlands, 8
Northern Rock, 3, 33, 40
nutrition label, 54, 58–65
"originate and sell" model, 13

Paulson, Hank, 5
pay caps, 78–79
Pension Protection Act of 2006, 55
pensions: defined benefit plans and,
53, 58; defined contribution plans
and, 53–55, 58, 61–63; retirement
savings and, 53–66
policy: bailouts and, 7–8, 79–82 (see
also bailouts); challenges of implementing, 149–52; clearinghouses and, 110–20; conflicts of
interest and, 16–21; credit default swaps (CDS) and, 109–21;
derivatives dealers and, 130–33;
different World Financial Crisis
scenario and, 140–49; executive
compensation and, 75–85; executory contract qualification and,
100–101, 106–8; hybrid securities
and, 89–94, 138; leverage and, 10,
14, 28, 87–90, 140–41, 146; liquidity and, 124–25, 138, 146; living
wills and, 96, 100, 103–5, 139, 144,
147–48; Pension Protection Act
of 2006 and, 55; prime brokers
and, 130–33; recapitalization and,
89–93, 138–39; reforming capital
requirements and, 67–74; regulation effects and, 2, 16, 25–26 (see
also regulation); resolution options and, 95–108; retirement
savings and, 53–66; runs and,
130–33; systemic risk and, 2, 19,
35–47, 50, 69, 74n1, 76, 81, 101,
105, 109–20, 137, 141–45; too-
big-to-fail, 18–19, 21, 29, 90; Troubled Asset Relief Program (TARP)
and, 5, 7, 83; two central principles of recommendations on,
135–40

policy scenarios: AIG and, 147–49;
Bear Stearns and, 142–44;
buildup of World Financial Crisis,
140–42; Fannie Mae and, 144–45;
Freddie Mac and, 144–45;
Lehman Brothers and, 145–47
politics, 150; consumer regulation
and, 37–38; Democrats and, viii;
executive compensation and, 80;
hybrid securities and, 92; Republicans and, viii
Posner, Richard, 43n1
prices: deflation and, 27; disruption
effects and, 11–12; fire-sale, 22,
31n14, 45–47, 51, 67–71; growth
effects and, 27; inflation and, 1,
41, 60, 65n2; information infrastructure for, 44–52; irrational
belief on, 27–28
prime brokers: assets and, 125–28;
client relationship and, 123; competitive market of, 124; default
risk and, 14–15; ethical issues
and, 126–27; hedge funds and,
123–30; information infrastructure and, 124; interest rate swaps
and, 128–29, 134n6; liquidity and,
122–32, 134n9; policy recommendations for, 130–33; regulation
and, 123–24; runs on, 4, 7, 10–11,
24–25, 122–33; segregated accounts and, 124–33; systemic risk
and, 130–33; United Kingdom and,
127–28, 132; United States and,
127–28
psychological biases, 57
put-call parity relations, 12
put options, 12, 31n12

race to the bottom, 124
recapitalization: conversion ratio and,
90–94; debt overhang and, 88;
expedited mechanisms for, 86–94;
hybrid securities and, 90–94; policy recommendations for, 89–93,
138–39; Tier 1 capital and, 92

recessions, 12–16, 29, 109, 141, 152
reform: capital requirements and, 67–74; clearinghouses and, 110–20, 139; credit default swaps (CDS) and, 110–20, 139; executive compensation and, 75–85; expedited restructuring mechanisms and, 86–94; external financing and, 68; short-term debt and, 68–69, 72–74
regulation, 2, 29; avoidance of, 16, 26; bailouts and, 137–40 (*see also* bailouts); broad vs. individual view of, 135–37; central banks and, 34, 38–43; consumer, 37–38, 42; costs of failure and, 137–40; covered interest parity and, 11; credit default swaps (CDS) and, 109–21; deposit insurance and, 23; executive compensation and, 75–85; financial markets and, 33–43; financial system problems and, 16–26; Futures Trading Commission and, 52; hybrid securities and, 35, 74n1, 89–94, 104, 138, 142, 146, 150; inadequate structure for, 25–26; individual institutions and, 33–34, 38; information infrastructure for, 44–52; innovation and, 26; legal impediments to, 96–97; leverage and, 10, 14, 28, 87–90, 140–41, 146; living wills and, 96, 100–101, 103–5, 139, 144, 147–48; political costs of, 37–38; principles underpinning policy recommendations and, 135–40 (*see also* policy); prime brokers and, 122–32; race to the bottom and, 124; resolution options and, 95–108; retirement savings and, 53–66; runs and, 123–24; Securities and Exchange Commission (SEC) and, viii, 5, 36–37, 40, 48, 52, 55, 142; sys-

temic, 33–43; TRACE system and, 118–20; U.K. style of, 37
Reinhart, Carmen, 29
Renaissance Technologies, 24–25
Republicans, viii
Reserve Primary Fund, 6, 25
resolution options: annual review of living will and, 105; bailouts and, 96–99; cross-country resolution process and, 99; executory contract qualification and, 99–100, 106–8; holding companies and, 95–97, 100, 104–5; hybrid securities and, 104; liability identification and, 97; living wills and, 96, 100–101, 103–5, 139, 144, 147–48; policy recommendations for, 99–100, 104–6; restructuring and, 95–108; runs and, 97–98
restructuring: bailouts and, 96–99 (*see also* bailouts); hybrid securities and, 89–94; liability identification and, 97; living wills and, 96, 100–101, 103–5, 139, 144, 147–48; planning for demise of major financial institution, 100–104; policy recommendation principles and, 136; recapitalization and, 86–94; resolution options and, 95–108
retirement savings: asset classes and, 65n2; automatic enrollment and, 62–63; back-end load and, 59–60; company stock limitations and, 63–64; consumer burden and, 53; costly mistakes in planning, 56–58; default options and, 54–55, 62–63, 66n4; defined benefit pension plans and, 53, 58; defined contribution plans and, 53–55, 57, 61–63; disclosure requirements and, 53–54; diversified investment and, 63; expense ratio and, 54, 59–60; financial illiteracy and, 57;

401(k) plans and, 53, 58, 65n1, 66n4; front-end load and, 59–60; high-fee funds and, 56, 59; information infrastructure for, 53–66; investment restrictions and, 54–55; Medicaid and, 56; moral hazard and, 56; mutual funds and, 54, 65n3; need for regulation of, 56–58; nutrition label model and, 54, 58–65; overconfidence and, 54; Pension Protection Act of 2006 and, 55; policy recommendations for, 58–64; psychological biases and, 57; regulation of, 53–66; self-discipline and, 57; standardized disclosure and, 53–55, 58–65; tax rates and, 57–58; Treasury Inflation Protected Securities (TIPS) and, 60; withholding rate and, 54–55, 62–63

risk: clearinghouses and, 110–20; counterparty, 45, 106–8, 110–13, 116–17, 120; credit default swaps (CDS) and, 109–20; default and, 1, 5, 8, 14, 29, 67–68, 71–72, 108n1; derivative positions and, 47–48; executive compensation and, 75–85; Federal Deposit Insurance Corporation (FDIC) and, 36, 41, 52, 88–89; fire-sale, 22, 31n14, 45–47, 51, 67–71; general asset positions and, 47–49; hybrid securities and, 90–94; information technology and, 28; liquidity and, 3, 10–12, 19–22 (see also liquidity); minimizing likelihood of bailouts and, 137–40; model-based valuations and, 50; prime brokers and, 130–33; psychological biases and, 57; recapitalization and, 86–94; reforming capital requirements and, 67–74; retirement savings and, 53–66; scenario of under recommended policy, 140–49; standard-

ization and, 35, 49–50; systemic regulator and, 33–43; Treasury Inflation Protected Securities (TIPS) and, 60

Rogoff, Kenneth, 29

runs, 5, 26–27, 29; classic, 23; conditions generating, 122–25; deposit insurance and, 23, 36, 52, 70, 88; Great Depression and, 23–24; liquidity and, 122–32; policy recommendations for, 130–33; prime brokers and, 4, 7, 10–11, 24–25, 122–33; regulation and, 123–24; Reserve Primary Fund and, 6; resolution options and, 97–98; secured creditors and, 23–24; self-fulfilling, 25; shadow banking system and, 9–12; Treasury bonds and, 23–24; vulnerability to, 97–98. See also bankruptcy

Scharfstein, David, 15

Securities and Exchange Commission (SEC), viii, 5, 37, 40, 48, 52, 55, 133n2, 142

segregated accounts: policy recommendations for, 124–25; prime brokers and, 124–33, 146; race to the bottom and, 124; U.S. rules on, 127

self-discipline, 57

shadow banking system, 9–12, 33, 37, 42, 136–37

shareholders, 151; bankruptcy resolution procedures and, 21–23; capital requirements and, 70; conflicts of interest and, 16–21; debt overhang and, 18; disciplining of financial institutions and, 138; executive compensation and, 79–81, 85n1; restructuring and, 87–88; segregated accounts and, 124–33, 146; troubled banks and, 87

short-selling, 5

Société Générale, 17
Squam Lake Group, vii–ix
Standard & Poor's (S&P) Index, 59, 147–48
standard disclosure: advertisement regulation and, 61–62; expense ratio and, 59–60; nutrition label model and, 54, 58–65; past returns and, 61; retirement savings and, 53–55, 58–65; risk measurement and, 60–62; simplicity for, 57–58
Switzerland, 8
systemic regulator: adequate resources for, 43; central bank and, 34, 38–43; consumer protection and, 42; crisis prevention and, 34–35; hybrid securities and, 35–36; individual institutions and, 33–34, 37; macroeconomic policy and, 38; policy recommendations for, 42–43; role of, 34–36; separation from other regulation and, 36–38; standardized position values and, 35
systemic risk, 2, 19; clearinghouses and, 109–20; credit default swaps (CDS) and, 109–20; executive compensation and, 76, 81; fire sales and, 22, 31n14, 45–47, 51, 67–71; information infrastructure and, 45, 47, 50; minimizing likelihood of bailouts and, 137–40; policy recommendations and, 137, 141–45; prime brokers and, 130–33; reforming capital requirements and, 69, 74n1; regulation effects and, 35–40, 42; resolution options and, 100

technology, 28
TRACE system, 118, 120
Treasury bills, 9, 72–73
Treasury bonds, 11–12, 23–24, 30n7, 65n2

Treasury Inflation Protected Securities (TIPS), 60
Troubled Asset Relief Program (TARP), 5, 7, 83

UBS, 8
United Kingdom: Her Majesty's Treasury and, viii; Northern Rock and, 3, 33, 39; prime brokers and, 127–28, 132; railway stocks and, 150; regulation style of, 37
United States, 139; asset backed securities and, 12–14; bankruptcy code and, 22; clearinghouses and, 115; contracted financial activity in, 12–16; credit crunch and, 12–16; golden parachutes and, 79; low savings rates in, 57–58; nutrition label model and, 54, 58–65; prime brokers and, 127–28; recession and, 12–16; reforming capital requirements and, 68; segregation rules in, 127; tax code of, 57–58
U.S. Congress, viii, 145
U.S. Federal Reserve, 3
U.S. Treasury Department, viii, 5; bank bailouts and, 7–9; equity investments and, 88; systemic regulation and, 41; treasury bonds and, 11–12, 23–24, 30n7, 65n2; Treasury Inflation Protected Securities (TIPS) and, 60

withholding rate, 54–55, 62–63
World Financial Crisis, vii–ix; agency issues and, 17–21; auction rate securities and, 3–4; bailouts and, 7–8 (see also bailouts); bankruptcy and, 21–23 (see also bankruptcy); Bernanke and, 5, 31nn14, 17, 89; clearinghouses and, 110–20; conflicts of interest and, 16–21; covered interest parity and, 11; credit crunch and, 7–9, 12–16,

30n1; credit default swaps (CDS) and, 109–21; default and, 1, 5, 8, 14, 29, 67–68, 71–72, 108n1; disruptions of normal pricing relations and, 11–12; economic welfare and, 1; executive compensation and, 75–85; financial system problems and, 16–26; Great Depression and, 1, 8, 16, 23–24; hybrid securities and, 35–36, 89–94; improving resolution options for, 95–108; information infrastructure and, 44–52; interbank lending and, 3, 6; living wills and, 96, 100–101, 103–5, 139, 144, 147–48; October 2008 and, 7–9; origins of, 26–29; prelude to, 3–4, 30n1, 140–42; preventing repeat of, 1–2; principles of policy recommendations and,

135–40; recapitalization and, 86–94; recession and, 12–16, 29, 109, 141, 152; reforming capital requirements and, 67–74; resolution procedures and, 21–23; restructuring and, 96–108; scenario of under recommended policies, 140–49; September 2008 and, 4–7; shadow banking system and, 9–12, 33, 37, 42, 136–37; sovereign debt and, 1; systemic regulation of financial markets and, 33–43; systemic risk and, 2, 19, 35–40, 43 (see also systemic risk); Troubled Asset Relief Program (TARP) and, 5, 7, 83; underestimated risk and, 28
World War I era, 26

Zhu, H., 116–17, 120n1